Financial Freedom –

the Alternatives' Way

Neil Ryder

Acknowledgements:

Yola O'Hara: Visually Explained

Juliet Platt: Tree Tops Communications

Ant Hodges: HodgesNet.com

Nicky Fitzmaurice: Satin Publishing

Disclaimer: Neil Ryder and My Goal Is are not qualified investment advisors and cannot provide personal investment advice. We act as agents for a number of alternative investment providers. We bring to the attention of our clients opportunities which we believe offer the potential for good financial return. We will guide you through the opportunity and the process. Where necessary, we will refer you to our business partners regarding other areas relating to an opportunity where we lack the knowledge and experience. We act, and you acknowledge that we act, as an agent/introducer to the product provider - we are not providing advice. We therefore do not take responsibility for any changes, charges or returns imposed by the provider within their contractual agreement with you. Where you feel necessary, it is important that you take independent financial and legal advice.

Neil Ryder and My Goal Is will not and cannot be held liable for any actions you take as a result of what you read here. In reading this guide you hereby indemnify both Neil Ryder and My Goal Is against any financial, health or other loss of any kind

Copyright © 2017 Neil Ryder – All rights reserved

Author Biography

Neil Ryder – For most of his working life Neil has exchanged his time for money – either as an employee or by being self-employed. Being employed or self-employed is the same thing. You just change who writes your salary cheque. Neil's faith in 'the system' was shaken when he hit his own financial crisis. At My Goal Is he is now set on taking control of his own financial future and is helping others to do the same.

Financial Freedom - The Alternatives' Way

Contents

	Warning!	1
	Introduction	3
	Neil's Story	4
	What is this book about	11
	How to use this book	13

Part One - The Principals

1	What is Financial Freedom	17
2	The Power of the Six Questions	23
3	How Do we recover our enquiring	33
4	Old thinking vs new thinking	39
5	Six 'honest serving' things you need to know	45
	Epilogue to section one	133

Part Two – Your Financial Freedom Journey Starts Here

6	Start your journey	137
7	What's your Story	139
8	Motivation: Why do you want to be financially free	143
9	Metrics: By when could you be financially free	169
10	Make money make money: What are you going to do to achieve financial freedom?	187
11	Means: How are you going to achieve financial freedom?	197

12	Mentors or meddlers: who do you need to help you?	235
13	Mobility: Where can I live	247
	Epilogue to section two	259
	Leap of Faith	261
	Glossary	264
	Further Reading and Next Steps	266

WARNING!

You are going to read things in these pages that you will find shocking and alarming. Your received understanding of the way money works is going to be significantly undermined as a result.

Prepare to be mentally and emotionally challenged.

Prepare to be shaken into an awareness that all is not as it would seem in the world of finance.

Finally, prepare to consider that you are being deliberately anaesthetised with misinformation and propaganda intended to keep you Just Over Broke in your JOB.

What lies between these covers is not for the faint of heart or the narrow of mind. You can cling forever to the crumbling ledge that is exchanging time for money, or prepare to take a leap of faith towards your financial freedom.

INTRODUCTION

If you've picked this book up and are in your thirties, congratulations! You have the opportunity to learn some secrets about making money work for you and to benefit from alternative ways to grow your personal wealth. This means that your 'retirement' – that is, the act of stopping exchanging time for money – could now only be years, rather than decades away.

What's more, you get to try ways of making money make money without reinventing any wheels, and without the same pitfalls I had to manoeuvre around. Since I'm old enough to be your father, there's lots of knowledge I'd love to impart in order to make your journey to financial freedom less fraught than mine was. And since I'm not actually your father, you might just follow my example!

If you're closer to sixty as you read this book don't worry. I began my financial freedom journey at the age of fifty-eight. Up until that point I had probably led a similar life to you – working hard through various jobs, always trying to earn more money, contributing regularly to a pension and paying increasing amounts of tax. Like most of us I got used to constantly feeling broke.

In the past five years, however, I have discovered a whole new world of possibility to make money make money and make better returns more quickly, to the extent that by the end of next year – only six years from when I set out on this journey – I anticipate being not only completely free of debt but also financially free to do whatever I want every day for the rest of my life. I'll repeat that: I will be debt free and financially free, able to live life as I choose, without worry or fear.

If this sounds like something you'd like to achieve, then read on. You don't need a pile of money to start with. You can do this starting with nothing. I'm going to show you how.

Neil's story

My name is Neil Ryder and for the past six years I have been helping ordinary people like you and me make better returns on their investments. I am sixty-four years of age and based in Royal Wootton Bassett in Wiltshire with my wife Christine, grown-up children Graeme and Emma, daughter-in-law Fay and grandson Zak.

There is really nothing special about me. I have spent my working life doing long hours, trying to earn more money and putting aside whatever I could into my savings and pension. I'm sure you've been doing pretty much the same thing.

What possibly makes me different from you is the decision I made in 2010 to stop blindly investing my pension money into equities in the hope the fund was going to support me and my family in my retirement.

The reason I made this decision was because one glance at my pension statements prompted a heart-sinking, panic-stricken realisation that sounded a bit like this (pardon the French): 'Oh Shit!'

What I learned following this realisation that there wasn't going to be enough money from my pension to live on, let alone enjoy life, and the subsequent decision to stop investing into my pension, is what I'm going to share with you in this book.

But first a bit more about me, just to show how normal I really am.

I grew up in the Midlands, a part of the UK dominated by the automotive industry. My Mom worked in a vehicle dealership and my Dad worked his way up from blue to white collar in the manufacture of car components.

So it stood to reason that when I left school at the age of nineteen I too should enter the automotive industry. Back in the 1960s that would have been a sensible, secure-seeming career path. My parents had both come from large families, which most probably influenced them to limit the number of children they produced, so I am an only child. Mom and Dad must have felt that they could give me the best start if I didn't have to compete with siblings. Their philosophy was the same as most people:

'Get a good education, get a good job and a good pension, and you're set for life.'

Unfortunately for me, and probably for you too, this would prove to be a fallacy.

I did well at school, and was considered to be in the top four per cent of ability when I passed my eleven plus to get a place at the King Edward Grammar School in Aston, Birmingham. I was surrounded by smart children who I thought would all go on to be leaders in their chosen careers.

After school I began a commercial apprenticeship with the AA (not Alcoholics Anonymous, the other one), continuing my family's link with the automobile industry. I was there for five years. I could have chosen to stay with that organisation and perhaps if I had I would have been in a job for life, with a great final salary pension. Yes, I would have had a secure career, but I would have missed out on a load of other experiences – and you certainly would not now be holding this book in your hands.

I guess I've always had a restless nature. At the age of twenty-four I wanted to move on to the next opportunity in my life. I was married and was looking to climb another rung on the career ladder. Like most young people, at that stage of my journey I did not give any thought at all about my pension benefits forty years down the line.

Throughout my early career I worked mainly in the car industry, primarily in sales and marketing roles. I've been made redundant and I've been given the sack, but I've never been one to dwell on the past. For that reason, I never attend school reunions: I never go back. I'm frequently disappointed to meet people from my past who are stuck doing the same thing they always did, and who didn't become the successful individuals I always thought they would.

In contrast, I feel as if I have made mistakes but I have done something with my life. In 1988 I got out of the corporate rat race to go it alone with my own consultancy business. At the time this felt like a bid for freedom and independence – to be my own boss and earn more money for myself rather than for my employer. However, the reality was that my clients became the boss of me, and I was necessarily limited not only by their budgets, but also by the amount of time I was able to dedicate to them.

While it may have seemed a good move to work for myself, the bottom line is that it didn't increase my freedom. I was missing out on time with my children, and my weekends were always clouded by thoughts of what I needed to do the following week. I was earning good money but I always felt blocked, and that I'd sold my soul. We were living very much the way most people live. Making more money meant we could have a bigger house, better cars, nicer holidays ... and more debt.

Gradually I began to see that this way of life is very much promulgated and promoted by the needs of the financial System. Employers, banks, Her Majesty's Revenue & Customs (HMRC) and the Financial Conduct Authority (FCA) all require people to earn money, acquire debt, pay taxes and invest cautiously. Money really does make the world of The System go round, and the more willing participants – you and me – the better.

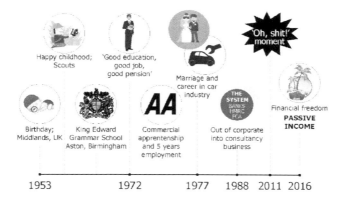

The penny was starting to drop. I could see that there was money to be made in the financial sector, but it was, and continues to be, heavily regulated, with the bulk of investment capital going into the equity market. The real wake-up call came for me when my wife Christine decided to retire.

In my family, all of the males are toy boys. I'm younger than my wife. Our son is younger than his wife. So Christine hit sixty a little under two years before I did. This was a spur for me to think 'I'd better dust off my pension statements and see where we stand.'

I pulled out ten years' worth of annual statements. You know the ones I mean. The ones that arrive every year, get opened and shoved into your sock drawer.

I was shocked to see that the only reason my pension fund had gone up in cash terms was because I'd been paying money into it every month – as I have done most of my life. The so-called 'expert' fund manager who was supposedly selecting the best equity returns for my money was adding nothing to my capital. This meant that the growth on my fund wasn't even keeping pace with inflation. In fact, it was going down in value.

Add to this the fact that I was still exchanging my time for money and still only just managing to ensure that I could cover the costs each month. After all, as our income increases we tend to spend it! Financial freedom was a long, long way off. Our financial future looked bleak; our retirement years would be nothing better than poverty-stricken unless I did something about it. In short, this was my 'oh shit' moment.

I did something about it. Six years after my wake-up call we're now just months away from financial freedom, with no debt, no real need to work anymore, and with a regular passive income that will allow us to do what we want to do every day without worrying about funding our lifestyle.

It was very tough at times, and there was a period where Christine and I were living on the edge, moving money around to cover our costs and acquiring a less than glowing credit history.

Nevertheless, I was learning a process which has enabled me to create a passive income of over £30,000 per month. (Yes you read that right.) I have honed and refined the necessary steps to the point that I now have clients who are benefitting from what I've learned and who are transforming their own financial futures. And now I'm going to share the secrets of that process with you so you can do the same.

What is this book?

This book originated as a forty page pamphlet I distributed to people I met at networking meetings. I used it to explain to them how I could help them satisfy their curiosity about financial freedom.

It was something I put together based on my own experience and my convictions about the need to improve our financial education in order to take control of our own money and future. It was intended to be an introduction to a new way of thinking, and a calling card for how I might be able to help people make progress in their own pursuit of financial security and independence.

When I first wrote the pamphlet I was two years into my own journey to financial freedom. At the time, following some passive income generating methods that I'm going to describe later in this book, I was already making a monthly income of around £10,000.

Happily, the pamphlet appealed to a number of people, who became clients. Since then, as I've worked with more clients I've both earned more and learned more. My monthly income has now trebled, and Christine and I are on track to achieve debt free financial freedom by the end of next year.

It's considered to be rather a rude question in polite society to enquire how people make their money.

However, I think it's important in the early pages of this book to give you some insight into my own situation.

When I engage with new prospects through My Goal Is, I am able to tell them quite candidly that I do not need their business. I make a considerable part of my income from my own investments. This means I do not need to charge for the coaching and mentoring services I provide to my clients. If having worked with me they decide to take advantage of any of the investment opportunities they learn about, then I receive a small introducer fee. This means I can tell my clients that I'd genuinely like to help them gain control of their financial future and make money work better for them. Although I charge nothing for the time I spend with people, the amount of coffee, cake and hospitality that some of my clients ply me with is suitable recompense!

The trouble is, I can only work with a limited number of people. Time and geography dictate who I can help. This book then is an attempt to reach and inspire more people. It tells my story, and the stories of some of my clients, and it contains some crucial principles by which I have learned to proceed.

My intention and hope is that this book sparks you to create the right conditions and opportunities to achieve your own financial freedom.

How to use this book

The book is split into two sections. The first is the reference section, in which I describe the current reality surrounding finance, as well as the mindset, principles and some of the necessary tools that are required to pursue your financial security, independence and freedom safely and responsibly.

A number of uncomfortable truths are revealed about how our minds deceive us and how we are conditioned to show obedience to The System — the prevailing financial, governmental and economic structure that needs us to operate in certain ways in order to sustain it. However, it is possible to break into a new way of thinking and adopt a set of principles with which to explore the new worlds that will open up for you.

The second section of the book is dedicated to you and your own process and journey to financial freedom. It contains specific information for you to consider as well as a series of questions and exercises for you to work through in order to move forwards confidently and securely into your financially free future.

There are frequent cross-references to the information contained in Section One, so you can flick back and refresh your understanding of various principles and tools as you work through. There are also blank pages left for your notes throughout the text, and a comprehensive glossary of key terminology at the back.

The longest journey starts with a single step – so step out and read on.

Your journey to Financial Freedom, the Alternatives' Way, starts here!

PART ONE

–

The Principles

1

What is financial freedom?

Before we go much further we need to be clear on where it is we're heading.

To be financially free fundamentally means you have no debt, no real need to work any more, and a regular passive income that will allow you to choose what you want to do every day without worrying about where the money is coming from.

In the past we have all tended to make several assumptions: getting a good education and a good job would give us the security we need; working hard would give us the independence we crave; and, finally, retirement would give us the freedom we desire. These are the standard lessons of The System. But we need to challenge them! (After all, The System wants us to exchange time for money for as long as possible.)

Once we begin the journey towards financial freedom by 'sacking the boss' and stopping the exchange of our time for money, we need different ways to define security, independence and freedom.

- *Security* means having enough regular income to cover your costs, although your income is still dependent on you (even with self-employment, which may represent many people's version of freedom and independence, you are still exchanging time for money). You are surviving but have little money for treats and luxuries.
- *Independence* means you are covering your costs and are beginning to create meaningful passive investments. You may still have some debt, but have sufficient funds to enjoy treats and luxuries.
- *Freedom* means you have no debt, and your income for the rest of your life comes entirely from passive investments. In this scenario, which is what this book is aiming to help you achieve, you have no need to work and when

you wake up in the morning you have complete freedom to choose what you want to do.

It's important that your income is passive in order to be truly free. Passive income is income that comes from investments that you have made that do not involve you in doing anything. Your money is earning money while you are asleep or sitting beside the ocean. If you have to do any sort of work in order to earn money, your time is not entirely your own and you are not entirely free.

But if you identify where your money can make money for you, you effectively generate for yourself an abundance of the next most precious commodity after your health: time to spend as you choose.

The present moment is all we have in life. It's the only moment we have in which to be and to do all we wish. And yet so many of us are unable to use it freely.

Imagine a bank that allocates you time every day to spend however you choose. Every day you have sixty seconds multiplied by sixty minutes multiplied by twenty-four hours – giving you 86,400 seconds each day. The only catch is if you don't spend them you can't carry them forward. Use them or lose them. Just imagine a bank that gives you 86,400 units to spend every day – but at the end of the day what you haven't spent you lose. If it was money, you'd make sure you spent it all ... but because it is time, how much of it do you waste?

Currently, the vast majority of us squander our seconds in service of exchanging time for money. The more money we wish to earn, the more time we believe we have to spend working. In direct consequence, we have fewer seconds left to ourselves and for those people and things we love.

Nevertheless, The System peddles us the myth that freedom will come eventually. The System calls it 'retirement'. But this is nothing but an illusion conveniently packaged to convince us to stay in the rat race and keep feeding The System what it needs.

I might sound cynical, but there are countless tragic stories of individuals who have worked hard throughout their lives, storing up cash for their retirement, only to drop dead pretty soon after giving up work. One widow described how she and her husband had been cheated of their freedom when he died suddenly shortly after retirement. They'd planned to go on cruises together, see more of the world outside the narrow confines of their hard-working lives, and had saved and dreamed hard to make their wishes come true. But it wasn't to be. Time ran out.

Maybe freedom isn't actually a state to be arrived at. Maybe it is rather a state of mind. Adopting this state of mind is an important first step on this path.

Summary

Financial freedom means:

- You no longer have to exchange time for money
- Challenging the myths and illusions of The System
- You can reclaim your time to do what you choose
- Your money is working for you rather than you having to work for money
- Your income is entirely passive

NOTES

[Page left blank for your reflections]

2

The power of the six questions

Since every book about freedom ought to have at least one poetic interlude, here's mine:

> I KEEP six honest serving-men;
> (They taught me all I knew)
> Their names are What and Where and When
> And How and Why and Who.
> I send them over land and sea,
> I send them east and west;
> But after they have worked for me,
> I give them all a rest.
>
> I let them rest from nine till five,
> For I am busy then,
> As well as breakfast, lunch, and tea,
> For they are hungry men:
> But different folk have different views:
> I know a person small—
> She keeps ten million serving-men,
> Who get no rest at all!
> She sends 'em abroad on her own affairs,
> From the second she opens her eyes—
> One million Hows, two million Wheres,
> And seven million Whys!
>
> Rudyard Kipling, *Just So stories*

Typical of a Cub Scout in the UK in the 1960s, my boyhood was heavily influenced by the creations of Rudyard Kipling. As a friend of Lord Baden-Powell, Kipling's *Jungle Book* characters suffused the Boy Scout movement and provided a vehicle around which boys could bond and create narratives for their adventures and deeds.

Later in my working life in sales and marketing, and subsequently in training, Kipling's influence continued, with the poem 'Six Honest Serving Men' becoming significant. It provided a useful structure to remember the six 'open' questions when speaking to prospects, encouraging long responses, in order to develop the fullest possible picture of their circumstances, motivations and obstacles.

These days, knowing what I know about The System and how it would have us work ourselves into the ground for little return, it's the second verse of the poem that is particularly poignant to me.

Here's why.

Financial education the world over is terrible. People are taught little more than The System's mantra of 'get a good education, then a good job with a good pension and you're set for life'. At the same time that The System is brainwashing us into being its economic slaves, we are gradually losing the insatiable curiosity we had as children, when we asked a million hows and seven million whys on a daily basis.

Even back at the turn of the twentieth century Kipling was highlighting how his own level of adult busy-ness had mitigated his desire to find things out, unlike the small person who never tires of enlisting the service of her questioning minions. Over a hundred years later nothing much has changed at all.

We all get mired in busy-ness and fulfilling our responsibilities, of whose importance The System constantly reminds us. As a result, we lose our 'beginners' mind' and our desire to enquire.

In a world where financial education is practically nonexistent, this lazy mindset eventually spells System-bound conformity and a constant struggle to stay just over broke through that so-called good job.

So Kipling's second verse is worth another look. We need to remind ourselves of our child-like questioning nature. This is the basis of learning. It is also the means by which parental or systemic ignorance can be exposed. Anyone who's ever had a child will know the awkward moment when you can no longer answer that final why in a sufficiently satisfactory way. This is when the child either gives up and accepts there are certain things not worth asking, or goes off to seek the answer for him- or herself.

The problem with education

Sometimes I wonder whether dropping out of school and becoming more self-reliant in one's education might produce better results.

Of course there is no justification for not trying, nor doing your best, at your studies. Please don't go advising your children to flunk their grades on purpose on the strength of what I'm about to say! But what I notice, and which ought to give consolation to parents whose children are struggling with their education, is that there is a huge number of highly successful entrepreneurs and business people who didn't break any academic records.

The tenets on which our school system is based are very familiar; they've been drummed into most of us since we were in short trousers and knee-length socks. 'Study hard, do well in your exams, get a good education, get a good job.'

It's tantamount to telling us to do as we're told. Good, compliant students will succeed; poor, noncompliant students will drop out.

But who's failing who?

Often the youngsters who fail their tests have a different type of energy and vision, which The System doesn't really know what to do with. Pupils who don't do as they're told end up in detention or, worse, get excluded altogether.

The really lucky ones might find a mentor to encourage them and help them along. Others will dream up their own schemes, and find out about things that The System isn't teaching them, like how to make and manage money, master new technology or run their own businesses.

In either case these youngsters have the nous to realise The System isn't really geared up to help them, so they figure out how to help themselves, and often set up their own enterprises at a very young age. We have to hope that these enterprises stay on the right side of the law!

A number of famous individuals have eschewed the education System to take control of their own destiny, and have been highly innovative and influential in their own right: Richard Branson is dyslexic and dropped out of school at sixteen to start his first two businesses in publishing and music mail order; John Lennon was kicked out of college; Bill Gates and Mark Zuckerberg both failed to complete their Harvard degrees; and Steve Jobs didn't even finish his first year of college before he left to found Apple.

Less lucky youngsters end up having to channel their energy somehow. They can get distracted by the wrong company and the wrong habits, which ultimately lead them astray and towards a future totally, and grudgingly, governed by the welfare system.

The other population of students will in the main get what's needed from their education to secure them a job, a salary and a tax code. At this point The System has them where it wants them: well and truly stuck in the rat race, paying taxes and living under the delusion that this is what 'success' is.

It's good to be inspired by those visionaries who bucked The System at an early age. They weren't getting what they needed from their education. They had more pressing things to be getting on with than getting their grades, so they got up and got on.

Perhaps this leads us to think that The System needs to change, to better accommodate or even encourage mavericks. Or perhaps this is where private education, with its smaller tutor groups, more time and greater capacity to harness different learning styles, succeeds in bringing the best out of young people.

In an ideal world, The System would improve the financial education it offers, so more individuals have the opportunity to understand as young people what is needed to become wealthy. How likely this is may be a moot point as The System still needs workers to sustain it. At the very least it could be better at helping people retain their enquiring mind, and not consign genuine curiosity to the dustbin.

If there are young people in your life you could serve them well by sharing with them what you are learning as you embark on your own journey to financial freedom, to show them they don't have to fall into the same trap as the majority of the generation before them.

Unfortunately, on matters financial we tend to have given up asking the questions. Instead we have been spoon-fed what The System wants us to swallow, and we are engaging in a universal game of working harder and harder in the mistaken belief that this is how to get rich. From the point of view of The System, it's better perhaps to propagate a culture of more modest, risk-averse aspirations, so people toe the line, pay their taxes and line the coffers of the financial industry.

The importance of mindset

As long as we have the mindset that waits to be filled up with propaganda, without enquiring into anything for ourselves, very little will change in our financial reality. As Edward De Bono remarked, we can't dig a different hole in a different place by digging the same hole deeper. If we want a different answer, we have to ask a different question. Or ideally six different questions, according to Kipling's Honest Serving Men.

How we think affects what we do. If we think The System is working, that it is giving us a fair return for our efforts, and that our earning potential is defined solely by our job, then it is unlikely we will be motivated to change our ways. But if we've experienced disillusionment and disappointment, then we at least have a chance to take a different approach.

When I realised that my pension fund wasn't keeping pace with inflation, and was only growing by virtue of the deposits I was making, I became aware of the flaws in The System that could have condemned Christine and me to a life of penury.

Luckily for us – and for you reading this book today – I didn't just accept what I was being told. I knew there had to be a better way, and I was determined to find it.

Summary

Taking the first step on the journey to financial freedom means:

- Rediscovering the power of child-like curiosity
- Reflecting on the shortcomings of your own and your children's financial education
- No longer accepting what you are being told
- Taking into consideration the children and young people in your life, and giving them the financial education The System won't give them.

NOTES

[Page left blank for your reflections]

3

How do we recover our enquiring mind?

Maybe you have always had a questioning nature and are finally turning that curiosity towards improving your financial situation before you reach crisis point. For me, the proverbial fan had already been hit before I had my Damascene moment that made me question everything. But for you, maybe things are different.

You might have been noticing that other people around you – a friend, a neighbour or a colleague – seem to have changed their circumstances. You might be noticing them going off on holiday quite a bit, or driving a brand new car or having the time to do more gardening. You might be wondering how they can afford to work less, yet still enjoy life's luxuries.

Meanwhile you are hard at the nine to five or longer, worrying about bills and pay rises and hoping your pension will be enough – but not really daring to think about it for too long.

How can they have shrugged off the rat race while you are still trapped in it? Have they won the lottery?

Come into an enormous inheritance? Or robbed a bank?

This is good. You are starting to question what might be going on for the people you are observing – but let's try not to jump to conclusions.

First off, it's highly unlikely that your neighbours have won the lottery. Honestly, the chances are one in fourteen million. Unfortunately, the phrase 'when I win the lottery' has become the scourge of many people's financial savvy since November 1994, when the UK National Lottery began. Listen carefully and you will notice that buying a lottery ticket every week is the sum total of many people's current wealth producing strategy. If you are one of them, it's time to stop right now!

If you want, you can consider how many pounds you have spent on lottery tickets since it began. I can tell you now that if you've bought a single ticket every week since then you have frittered away over £1200.

'So what?' you might say. Until you find out that your neighbours decided on a different strategy for their lottery pound a week. Hence, they are now living the life of Riley.

OK, it is possible that your neighbour has inherited a handsome stash from a long-lost relative.

Nevertheless, it surely cannot be enough to completely give up work, meet existing financial commitments *and* maintain the lifestyle they currently have. How long is that going to last? Are they quietly blowing the whole lot without realising they will face penury once it's all gone?

Your own worst enemy

You may have caught yourself saying to your partner: 'They'll be sorry in the long run when the money runs out and they're too old to go back to work.'

This is jealousy – and it's not attractive.

Another version might be: 'Well it's all right for them but it's not what I'd choose to do.'

That's slightly better than jealousy. But it's still what losers say.

So stop that too. If you carry on with that sort of narrative you are only going to do one thing, and it will be the most damaging thing you can do to your emerging financial curiosity.

Here's what it is: You are going to talk yourself into thinking you're right.

And then you're going to reinforce your self-righteousness by telling all your rat race friends about your mad neighbours, and one of your friends who works in the financial industry will suck their teeth and shake their head and make you feel even more validated in your judgement, because they have a professional opinion.

So all that will happen is you will close down, and not learn anything new, and stay trapped in the nine to five.

Alternatively, you might convince yourself that they must have robbed a bank. I'll leave you to decide what you would do in that Walter Mitty scenario. (I'm envisaging more the risk of you being sectioned than the likelihood of a helicopter raid on your neighbourhood.)

Trust me, there is a simpler answer.

If you feel that, yes, you are that person who wants to know how other people give up work and spend their days doing whatever they want – Congratulations! You have attained the first rung on the same ladder of financial freedom that your neighbours have climbed.

How come?

Quite simply because you are beginning to question what they're doing – and as long as you keep an open mind, and don't get sidetracked by jealousy or self-righteousness or 'professional opinion', it won't be too long now before you start to question what *you're* doing, too.

And once you start questioning, you are ready to begin your financial education. Go back and read the poem. What, When, Why, Who, How and Where are going to become loyal servants of yours, and you are going to learn some stuff that will completely transform your life.

Summary

Preparing your mindset for financial freedom means:

- Questioning everything you've been told with genuine curiosity and a desire to understand
- Keeping an open mind
- Giving up being your own worst enemy.

NOTES

[Page left blank for your reflections]

4

Old thinking vs new thinking

Take a look at the following table, demonstrating the characteristic mindset of someone who is bound by The System, compared with the attitudes of someone keen to do things differently.

Notice how both ways of thinking use the six question words – but to very different effect.

Old thinking – for System conformity	New thinking – for possibility
When I win the lottery …	By when do I wish to achieve my dream?
Who's died? Who's left them some money? Who do they think they are? Who can I blame? Who do I think I am?	Who can help me? Who has already achieved financial freedom – and how can they help me to do the same? Who must I talk to?
What are they thinking blowing all that money/giving up work/taking early retirement? What on earth am I going to do?	What is my current financial situation? What steps can I take to improve my situation straight away? What strategies are available to grow my wealth from this point?

Why bother?	Why is it important to me to grow my wealth? Why do I want to change my financial reality?
How the hell am I expected to afford that? How can it not be a scam? How am I meant to believe that? How much harder must I work?	How can I afford to make my dream a reality? How can I reinvest my pension? How can I make my money work harder? How does the power of compounding work? How can I be sure it's not a scam? How can I mitigate my risks?
Where's the money tree? Where am I going to find that sort of money? Where's the bank they robbed? Where do I buy a winning lottery ticket?	Where do I want to live/work/spend my holidays? Where shall we take the children this summer? Where's a good place to buy property?
Old thinking keeps you stuck, judgemental and defeated.	*New thinking helps you make progress, take action, make your dreams a reality.*

Which side of the table do you most identify with? Go on – be honest! How many times have you caught yourself asking the facetious, rhetorical questions of the old way? How does it feel to glance over the positive action questions of the new way?

The Six Honest Serving men are great guides throughout your journey. You need them to get started, and you need them along the way to build connections, create opportunities and ensure the viability of investment schemes that are offered to you.

The first lesson in becoming financially free is learning how to ask different questions. But there are some things to be mindful of.

First of all, once you start to question what you've been systematically told it may lead you to question your beliefs and your values. If you're used to a mindset more akin to the old way of thinking, you could experience quite a lot of resistance to taking on a new outlook and approach.

Furthermore, it can sometimes be difficult, especially in this Information Age, to differentiate between opinion and fact. Certain information on websites and in the Press is presented as fact, and comes with a stamp of authority simply by virtue of its having been published. In order to navigate this, we need to flex another muscle – that of diligence. Although we need to rebuild our child-like curiosity, we must not fall into the gullibility trap. We need to be able to distinguish between propaganda and fact.

The limitations of the finance industry

A key question to ask to get to the heart of the propaganda matter is 'Whose interests are being served?' Or 'Who is subsidising this information?' For example, it is interesting to reflect on how the Financial Conduct Authority is funded. The FCA is lauded in popular understanding as the investors' safety net. It's a role that it plays very well, as the recent pension changes demonstrated. Anyone considering changing their pension arrangements receives a cautionary leaflet, emblazoned with a black, shiny scorpion, and with all the attitude and rhetoric of old thinking.

In effect this leaflet is a warning shot over the bows of independent thinkers wanting to make their money make more money. Such action would reduce the reliance of investors on equities, and therefore on the pension fund managers and independent financial advisors who act as funnels for such investment strategies. The wrinkles appear when you understand that the FCA regulates the equities investment market, and that it is funded in part by the organisations and institutions it regulates. Hmm.

So, although it poses as such, the FCA isn't really a safety net for investors as much as for its own funding stream. All is not as it seems.

The best course of action is to arm yourself with the Six Honest Servants, and use them with open-minded diligence, taking nothing at face value.

You are beginning an explorative journey and are creating in yourself an ability to ask the necessary, innocent questions to build a framework for new knowledge.

Summary

Building a framework for new financial knowledge means:

- Learning to ask different questions
- Being prepared to question your own beliefs and values
- Differentiating fact from opinion
- Beginning to understand the role, motives and limitations of financial professionals

NOTES

[Page left blank for your reflections]

5

Six 'honest serving' things you need to know

Why does our mind play tricks on us?

When it comes to determining our level of financial independence, it's worth reflecting on our human tendency to believe in illusion rather than reality. As a young adult, becoming financially independent means getting your first pay cheque, and not having to ask your Mum and Dad for a loan to buy the things you need or do the things you want.

But is this *real* independence?

As life goes on the things we *want* to buy and the things we *want* to do increase, largely to compensate for the things we *have* to buy and the things we *have* to do.

We have taxes to pay; as well as mortgage repayments, credit card bills, car loans, utility costs, subscriptions, school fees and living expenses to cover.

At this stage we are big enough and ugly enough to do our own tax return, fill out our own credit applications and provide for our dependants. We have become 'economically active'. We have been allocated a National Insurance Number, a Unique Tax Reference (UTR) and a place on the electoral roll. But does this mean we have achieved financial independence?

No.

Suddenly we are dependent on our employer, banks, credit card and loan companies to fund our needs and desires. All we have done is transfer our financial dependence from the Bank of Mum and Dad to one or two on the High Street. What's more, because this is something that the majority of people do, we collectively create the illusion that this is the right and only way to go about things.

The more pressured by obligation and responsibility we become, the more we choose to try to buy ourselves out of the stress of it all with treats, gadgets, cars, houses and holidays.

The trouble is we then discover that we cannot buy our escape. This is partly because what we really need, money cannot buy. It's also partly because we're using a false escape route that tends to take us into more debt, more obligation and more dependence. We have bought into an illusion of financial independence and are cheating ourselves of the reality of our situation. We are locked in!

Perhaps we'll become financially independent – and less deluded – when our income is generated entirely by ourselves.

This is getting warmer. But, even in the scenario where we are self-employed, we are still dependent on what we do ourselves to get paid. You are still reliant on a 'boss' to pay you, even though that boss might be you!

True financial independence begins when we acquire the one significant thing that money cannot buy, namely real financial literacy. Only then can we settle our debts, spend less than we earn, 'sack the boss' and start making money work for us instead of the other way around.

Having already established one of the illusions we subscribe to about financial independence, why do we keep falling for this illusion?

How our minds are trained

From a young age we are trained to accept certain illusions as truth. It starts when we're very small. Think about how we teach our children to believe in

Father Christmas or the Tooth Fairy. On the one hand you might describe this as the magic of childhood. On the other hand, it might feel like manipulative conditioning.

'You have to be a good little boy otherwise the Tooth Fairy won't come'; or 'You'd better write your letter to Santa and tell him what a good little girl you've been.'

Have you ever said things like this to your children? Once you think about it, it makes you cringe a bit, doesn't it?

The other way we train ourselves to fall for illusion over reality is by answering our children's questions in a way that may or may not present real, truthful information to them, but which at least lets us off the hook. Whatever we tell our young children they will completely believe, so we really ought to be careful how we answer their questions. It can be difficult when they go on and on with their endless curiosity while you're trying to concentrate on something else. It's very tempting to tell them anything just to give them something to think about and get them to be quiet. But actually when we understand that we are in danger of giving them a piece of misinformation that might be illusory, and that might shut them up out of fear, then our impatience starts to look very cruel.

So we need to be careful what we tell them. But our tendency to believe illusion over reality doesn't end when we are children. As humans we have the capacity to continue choosing illusion over truth throughout our adult lives, particularly where we feel emotional, vulnerable or insecure.

Our biggest obstacle

We all build a picture of what we want and start to think about how we're going to get there. Then the mind starts to put obstacles in our way to protect us and prevent us from doing anything that might hurt us. Such mind-generated fear is our biggest obstacle.

Typically, what happens for many people is that, swayed by the rationalising threats of their over-cautious mind, they talk themselves out of their ideal situation and consign it to the scrap heap alongside everyone else's pipe-dreams. Suddenly it feels impossible to see how they might achieve what they would most like to do, so they retreat into what they know and where they feel most comfortable.

It is no coincidence that the comfort zone of many individuals comprises getting a good education, getting a good job and paying their taxes. No coincidence, because this is the message we've been hearing for generations through our schooling and our parents. This is the message of The System, which requires our fear-driven compliance in order to sustain itself.

One of the most emotive aspects of modern life that can hold us in the grip of fear is the subject of money. It stands to reason therefore that money is a topic about which many of us choose to believe comforting, illusory things rather than confront the reality of it.

As a result, we might not get to know our own financial situation very well. At worst we might run up debt on our credit cards, believing the illusion that as long as we pay off the minimum amount every month we are free to spend as much as we like.

At best we might assume that we don't have any capital or savings or pension – only to discover, on better understanding our true circumstances, that we can already create opportunities for greater wealth from amongst our existing assets.

Of course, taking all of The System's propaganda as the gospel truth, rather than something to challenge and get curious about, is one of the biggest causes of illusory living. Our fears about financial insecurity, lack of income and poverty in old age all conspire against us asking any questions of The System we've been conditioned to contribute to and rely on.

But once we get to know how easy it is to get our minds to fall for illusions, we can start to play this to our own advantage. As you work through this book you will discover how you can use the illusory powers of your brain to create the success you desire, and then work out the steps you can take in reality to get you there.

As the Chinese proverb reminds us, it all starts with one single step. Let the first step you take bring you closer to the reality of your situation, and away from the illusions of The System.

Summary

Our mind can play tricks and prevent us from achieving our full potential because:

- It is trained to accept illusions as truth
- It wants to keep us safe and comfortable
- It's afraid of being different

NOTES

[Page left blank for your reflections]

What is holding us back?

We cannot blame ourselves entirely for any lack of progress we may be experiencing. We need to cut ourselves a little bit of slack. We also need to recognise that there are social, educational, financial and political factors – collectively referred to here as The System – that conspire with our fearful minds in order to block our path to freedom.

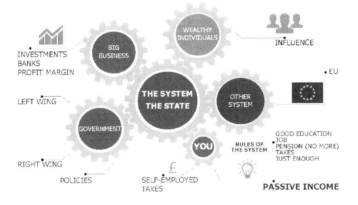

The System comprises a number of co-dependent groups. These include politicians, the State, big business, and wealthy and influential individuals.

The politicians wish to appeal to individuals' hearts and minds, so will introduce policies that are attractive to their electorate. Depending on the ruling party, these will include either greater freedom or greater constraint regarding personal wealth, enterprise and benefits. To a certain extent the ideology of the politicians is tempered by the State, which must maintain The System.

Big business, such as banks and financial houses, are interested in maintaining their own profit margins, and paying their shareholders. They are wealthy enough to fund their own regulatory body to ensure that their services are promoted and protected.

Wealthy and influential individuals each have their own agenda for their own and others' wealth, and will use their influence to pursue this. The System is as dependent on these people as they are on it.

Our place in The System

We each have a vital role to play in the maintenance of the immediate financial system in which we participate. For UK tax-payers this includes our employer, HMRC, Central and Local government. We each have to play by the rules of The System, in order not to attract attention to ourselves and incur penalties.

In return, if we work hard, get a good education and secure the best employment, we are able to buy a home, raise our families, pay our taxes and our dues, and have just enough money left over to live on.

Providing we comply, The System doesn't bother us or interfere with our lives.

This is certainly the main credo of the majority of people in the UK, who are all settling for 'just enough', or possibly less, in order to live 'right' within The System. Most people accept their lot and consign their life's dreams and aspirations to the dustbin, largely because they have been either brainwashed or frightened, or both, by a system which needs compliant individuals in order to sustain itself.

Benefits of The System

One of the reasons why people are so compliant is because The System appears to recognise that some people need greater flexibility in order to thrive.

For example, The System supports entrepreneurs to establish limited companies through incentives and benefits such as tax and expense allowances. In the property arena, buy to let landlords have been allowed to offset interest against income; and small businesses can enjoy Value-Added Tax breaks up to a certain amount of turnover.

Putting the brakes on

However, like any system, whenever there is the chance that its homeostatic stability is under threat, it must take corrective action. In the human body the pancreas controls blood sugar levels through the production of insulin; in financial systems the bureaucrats control the input of currency through the creation of taxable events.

So in the realm of property investment, as from 1 April 2016 not only have landlords faced a higher stamp duty tariff on the purchase of rental properties, they have also seen a change over the next five years as to how much of their mortgage interest payments they can offset against their income.

Furthermore, from 6 April 2016 company dividends beyond £5000 are now taxed at 7.5 per cent for basic rate tax payers.

The bottom line is that The System doesn't want individuals to earn too much money without being able to take a slice.

Could we ever escape The System?

Here at My Goal Is we are delighted that more and more people are keen to escape the time for money trap. We are here to help individuals learn about how they can achieve their own financial freedom, and to act as a signpost for opportunities they might wish to explore.

However, the financial System that makes the world go round is a much bigger, hungrier beast. Our escape from its all-consuming grip is likely to be rather more challenging.

People who have worked hard for much of their lives for little personal wealth are beginning to wake up to the downside of The System, which keeps us just over broke in jobs and liabilities. And, as people discover more about entrepreneurship, assets, alternative investment opportunities and passive income streams, there is a growing awareness that there is another way to make money work for us – rather than the other way round.

As people begin their exploration, they begin asking challenging questions.

Naturally when people's curiosity is piqued they will search high and low for information to feed their questioning minds. The Internet is the place to gorge on stories, reports, videos, documentaries and points of view from all sides of the spectrum of interest. During the education process individuals will come across speakers, coaches, consultants, authors, bloggers, mentors and media-savvy entrepreneurs whose message is powerful and compelling, and whose content is slick and expertly presented. It is a heady mixture of myth-busting, factual analysis and motivational broadcasting. And it's entirely up to the individual which one of the gurus' styles is most appealing to them. But be aware whose pockets you are lining as you progress your education.

One such video series – *The Hidden Secrets of Money* – has recently been brought to our attention by a client of ours. Its producer and host is an interesting guy named Mike Maloney, who is very well-read, very knowledgeable and a consummate communicator.

In one of the videos Mike exposes governmental spending, the raising of taxes and the generation of currency as one of the biggest scams in the history of mankind. It makes fascinating viewing, albeit a tad depressing, and prompted our client to get in touch with a question:

'If currency is nothing more than an artificial construct, what are the best assets to invest in now?'

(Mike Maloney is the CEO of goldsilver.com – so I guess he'll have some particular recommendations about investible assets!)

The difficult truth is that while currency may be an artificial representation of wealth, at the moment it is all we have. Even though we can take steps to escape the time for money trap, we cannot unfortunately free ourselves from the currency system. There is nowhere 'off-grid' to go. Not yet.

We can't change The System. All we can do is make it work for us. We know we can stop exchanging time for money and make money make money, so we have to enjoy it while we can.

The other way to look at it is to believe that the majority of people are creative and are fundamentally motivated by things other than money.

One of the most striking things about people who escape the time for money trap is how quickly they want to give back as soon as they start feeling that they have empowered themselves outside the established System. Either through giving to charity or giving their time, many people become altruistically motivated when they feel financially secure.

So perhaps this is how change will come about. As people free themselves financially, so they free their minds and creativity to dream up the 'off-grid' solutions. It happened with energy, so it could happen with money too.

We are in transition. We cannot tell when or if The System will collapse, nor what will replace it. But we can be part of the movement to become better educated, more secure and free from the rat race.

Summary

The System holds us back because:

- It needs to preserve economic, social and political homeostasis
- It cannot tolerate people making too much money without taking a slice
- It conspires with the insecurities of our mind to lock us in
- It works hard to make us believe that there is no alternative

NOTES

[Page left blank for your reflections]

NOTES

[Page left blank for your reflections]

How will you escape?

Exchanging your time for money in a JOB that keeps you Just Over Broke is a central pillar of the rat race. It's what the majority of people are doing and it means that you have little control over your days. After a while this level of financial security might begin to feel more like imprisonment.

As you begin to generate replacement income through property, investments and other passive means, you get to the position where you have sacked the boss and perhaps have become self-employed.

You are beginning to achieve financial independence. Your money is not entirely dependent on your time, but you may not be debt free. Also all you have really done is change the name of the boss who signs your pay cheque! Remember, self-employment still involves exchanging time for money.

You can declare yourself financially free when your income is generated entirely from passive investments – *and* you're free of debt.

Be aware that to properly escape the rat race you have to drop rat race thinking. This sort of thinking is founded upon the received wisdom that financial success is contingent upon a good education, a good job and a secure pension. It is also prone to the mentality that causes teeth sucking and eye rolling and that peculiar sing-song voice saying 'If it looks too good to be true it probably is.'

If you wish to defeat the stranglehold of the old way of thinking, you need to stop falling for this type of entreaty. How long it takes you to get through each stage of your financial freedom journey is dependent upon your own shift in thinking and how much you turn back to the propaganda of The System.

Who are you becoming?

As you leave behind your rat race network you will become a victim of others' envy. You are embarking on a different learning process and beginning to create a new social network. Don't be surprised if you encounter jealousy – but don't be swayed by others' opinions. Freedom is about choosing to be free from the illusions of The System, and of well-meaning friends, family and colleagues. It's about choosing not to conform; and it's about being immune to the effects of other people's judgement.

It is famously considered vulgar to discuss religion and politics in polite company – and money runs a very close third in the rankings of taboo topics. Boasting about money is obnoxious; complaining about a lack of money is similarly odious. No one really wants to know.

The only time it is at all acceptable to discuss money is when you are talking about ways to make it – and only then with people who share your motivation, and who can either advise you from their experience, or ask for your advice.

So before you embark on your journey into financial education there is an important thing you must be prepared for: you might lose some friends.

Not everyone believes that financial freedom is possible. If you count amongst your existing social circle those whose financial reality and aspirations are stuck in the routine of working, paying tax, saving a little and spending the rest, then it is unlikely you will have many stimulating discussions about investment returns, deal opportunities and passive revenue generation.

What is likely instead is a lot of teeth-sucking, head-shaking and pooh-poohing of any topic that touches on personal wealth.

Much of this behaviour is borne out of ignorance, fear and a reluctance to take any path deemed riskier than the status quo i.e. *any* path. For many people the tried and trusted philosophy 'better-the-devil-you-know' is the only viable approach to personal wealth management. This will prove tiresome for both parties over a prolonged period. Perhaps many awkward supper times, pub chats and coffee catch-ups will ensue, during which you become increasingly circumspect about the topic of money. Perhaps money will ultimately become the intolerably uncomfortable elephant in the room, squashing the life out of your friendship.

At this point there are two stark choices. Either shut up, or find new friends.

Happily, if you are keen to explore how to increase your personal wealth, and are genuinely interested in learning more about financial independence, there are lots of people who are also treading that same path, and who would be delighted to help you along.

Once you achieve the calm, well-informed, peace of mind that you are on a path towards your financial freedom and your true potential, you are untouchable.

Nevertheless, your behaviour throughout this process is vital. Are you going to become the arrogant so-and-so who treats people like dirt? Or are you going to put your wealth to good effect, not only to enhance your own quality of life, but to give back to others too?

Financial education and freedom brings with it a huge opportunity for personal development too. Understanding that everyone is genuinely doing the best they can do with the resources they are given will go a long way in tempering any feelings of entitlement just because you're rich enough to qualify for valet parking. And don't forget karma. It would be a shame to get a big scratch down the side of your Ferrari!

Escaping the rat race for myself and Christine has meant that we have changed our relationship with time. We have become the masters of it. And now, when we wish to plan a theatre trip, a holiday or a weekend away it's no longer a question of *if* we've got the money, it's now much more a question of *when* we can go. We are able to take a much more leisurely approach to planning our time, and there is no question of missing anything because we will have planned and funded it far enough in advance. There's a horrible frantic feeling about life in the rat race, when you feel like you have to grab the bargains or miss out. It's like the crush of the January sales or Black Friday. These days we don't need to experience that – and in some ways that's what freedom should be about.

Our perception of the value of money is changing too. Eighteen months ago £500 would have seemed like a phenomenal amount of money. Now, £500 is the bill for a really good night out in London, including dinner, a show and a hotel.

I'm not an extravagant person, but the fact is that I am now able to choose how to spend my money.

Suddenly we're doing things that I would personally have perceived as extreme or extravagant, and that perhaps others still do.

Although I don't worry about spending this quantity of money, thanks to my conditioning and the way I was brought up I do still feel guilty. I know this is a symptom of old thinking rearing its ugly head, but in some ways perhaps this is a good thing. It is a reminder of things that once upon a time we daren't take for granted. Part of our level of comfort around our increased wealth is to be grateful for what we have achieved, to behave decently and not to be too flash.

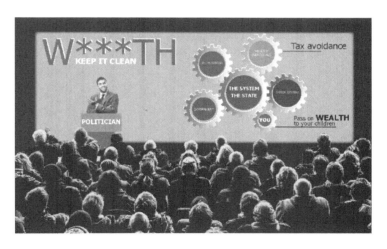

Summary

Escaping the rat race means:

- Embracing your own potential for wealth
- Turning your back on the propaganda of The System
- Receiving others' judgements like water off a duck's back
- Paying attention to who you are becoming

NOTES

[Page left blank for your reflections]

When will you achieve your dream?

There are three things you need to consider at this point in your journey.

- Firstly, how long do you have to reach your goal? When's your 'by when' date?
- Secondly, what resources do you have – cash, assets, savings/pension?
- Thirdly, what is your attitude towards risk?

If you're in your mid-thirties with a regular income, a house and a growing pension fund and you're looking at a planning window of up to twenty-five years to 'retire' with a million pound pension pot, then you have a fair amount of time to play with.

This will likely influence the third factor in the equation – that of your attitude to risk. If you have twenty-five years and plenty of resources you will probably have a low attitude to risk, meaning you would prefer to take low risk strategies with your money.

On the other hand, if you are in your late fifties and looking to retire before you're sixty-five but you don't have an enormous pension pot and you have limited assets, then your attitude to risk will necessarily have to be fairly aggressive if you wish to live in the manner to which you have become accustomed. This means that you will have to consider some 'higher risk' investments in order to get you where you want to be.

What route will you take?

The table below illustrates the profiles of some of my clients, with particular emphasis on the resources available to them, the timescale they are working to and their attitude to risk. These are the key pieces of information you need to determine the most likely route you might take to financial freedom.

Who	Resources	Time	Attitude to risk	Outcome
Juliet and Andy (mid to late 40s)	Cash + Pension + House (mortgage free)	*15 years to retirement *2 years to covering expenses passively	Medium	*Invested cash to achieve partial income within 60 days *Pension growing 20% pa *House remains mortgage free
James (early 40s)	House	*Less than 6 months after leaving a high pressure job	High	*Invested cash to replace income
Eva and Pete (mid 40s)	Cash + House	*2–3 years dropping to 18 months	Medium	*Invested cash to give income *Invested in property as a capital asset
Mike (early 40s)	Cash	*15 years to retirement *Five Year Plan to achieve	Medium	*Invested cash to achieve partial income within 60 days *Immediate increase in savings interest *Interest payments covering the cost of his wedding in 2016

How long will it take *you* to achieve your goal of financial freedom?

In order to work it out you need to analyse the key factors for yourself.

As the table above illustrates, the combination of resources you have, your attitude to risk and the timescale you are working to are interlinked and will determine what is possible for you over what period of time.

If you have a pressing need right now to address any shortfall in your pension, savings or capital, you are going to have to adopt a higher level attitude to risk in order to drive your decisions in the short term. If you do not choose higher risk investments, you are unlikely to make the returns you require to rectify your shortfall and provide ongoing income into your future.

This is the case for James. He had to leave his job for health reasons, but he needed to make sure he could cover his expenses straight away. His timescale was tight and his resources were limited to his house. Circumstances forced him to adopt a high risk attitude and he made the radical decision to release the capital from his house and invest the cash to generate a replacement income immediately. He has now chosen to live in rented accommodation, but has managed to sack the boss and choose his own work.

Eva and Pete's case is interesting. Their dream was to own and run a retreat centre abroad. Once they had carried out a full appraisal of their resources, and determined they had a medium risk attitude, they were able to achieve their dream in half the time they had anticipated.

What do we mean by risk?

Typically, when we think of high risk investments we think about scams. Think Ponzi Schemes, which don't have any sort of underpinning asset and whose returns are dependent entirely on the investment capital of others in the scheme. That is – your returns *only* come from the contributions of other investors, not from real asset growth.

In 1920 in Boston, Massachusetts, Charles Ponzi attracted thousands of dollars of investor money into his scheme, supposedly trading cheap, foreign International Reply Coupons for profit back in the US. He promised that investors would make a 100 per cent return in ninety days, and money poured in.

The perpetual flow of capital enabled Ponzi to fulfil his promised returns from new investors' money, effectively robbing Peter to pay Paul. In actual fact, Ponzi did nothing to trade the coupons and generate any kind of genuine profit.

A similar, though more sophisticated, scheme was busted in the States in 2008, this time landing its organiser Bernie Madoff behind bars for a total of 150 years.

Ponzi Schemes are characterised by the promise of high returns and appear to be immune to market volatility. They are also devoid of any profit-generating asset. Alarm bells should ring. These schemes are without doubt fraudulent scams.

For anyone whose financial understanding relies upon either the media, the regulated financial industry or the consumer banking sector, any investment opportunity that offers a higher-than-the-High-Street return might be quickly dismissed as a Ponzi Scheme or a scam.

The father of one of my clients is retired from the National Health Service, and is now drawing income from a government-run medical pension. Recently my client was attempting to explain to him some of the asset-backed Alternative Investment opportunities we use here at My Goal Is

My client explained that during the course of their conversation the phrases 'Alternative Investment' and 'higher-than-High-Street returns' elicited much teeth-sucking and knotting of brows from the former surgeon.

'It sounds like a Ponzi,' he uttered at last.

My client reflected for a moment, and said, 'I've heard of that before. Isn't it a Scheme where all pay-outs are from the capital put in by fellow investors, rather than from the returns of a profit-generating asset?' My client wanted to be sure they were referring to the same thing.

She then went on, 'I've also heard that in that type of Scheme even some innocent third parties might be having their money hived off to top up the fund, and so guarantee pay-outs for the Scheme's members!' (My client might have been getting just a little carried away with the satire.)

'If that's the case,' she explained, 'a government-run, taxpayer-subsidised, non-asset-backed NHS pension sounds like a Ponzi too!' At this point I'm sure my client, who isn't a cruel person, thanked her father for his concern and gave him an affectionately reassuring nudge.

Just because something produces a high return on investment doesn't mean it's a Ponzi Scheme. Basic due diligence on any investment opportunity can quickly determine the reliability of the projected return, and whether the underpinning asset is genuine.

By the way, the banks don't want you to know that overnight they are trading your money without telling you. They could be making as much as one per cent *a night* on their customers' deposits – returns that enable them to pay their overheads, bonuses, taxes and shareholder dividends. Meanwhile they pay you interest of one per cent *per annum* (if you're lucky) out of what's left. No wonder then that they want you to believe that you've got to put your savings and investments into High Street schemes, and continue accepting measly returns.

The lesson here is not to fall for so much misinformation surrounding investment opportunities and dismiss them as Ponzis. You could be missing a huge chance to make your money work a lot harder for you than it can on the High Street. If you do, financial freedom will forever elude you.

Of course, Ponzis and scams are the types of scheme to be avoided, and that the FCA and other advocates of The System quite rightly warn us against. However, the warnings extend beyond these types of scam into anything that lies beyond the boundaries of *whole of market*. This is because the regulated institutions of The System cannot make any money out of investors interested in growing their wealth outside of these boundaries. So anything that is not within the specific *whole of market* catchment, namely anything which is defined as an Alternative Investment, is automatically classified by The System as High Risk.

The risk associated with investing can be mitigated substantially by being clear on the type of opportunity you are looking at and understanding what the underpinning asset is that will generate growth; and what the returns are over what period. You also need to protect your capital at all costs, by ensuring you can retrieve it in full through a capital guarantee or through a first charge over the asset. Ironically, the vast amount of whole of market opportunities represented by regulated financial institutions are equity based and do not offer these guarantees. They are subject to the volatility of the markets.

Essentially it is not accurate to dismiss a high returning opportunity as high risk purely on the strength of its promised returns.

Your own attitude to risk is an important thing to be aware of and define for yourself. But even more important is that it is informed. You also need to know that our individual approach to risk is mutable and does change over time. As we get older our attitude to risk may decrease or increase depending on our circumstances and the urgency of the need to improve our financial situation. We might choose to plod on into penury – or we might also choose to take some radical action and give ourselves and our lives a financial boost.

Having a very clear picture of what your resources and timeframe are will further inform what action you can take. Completing the Financial Freedom Planner in Section Two is the first step, as well as determining what you wish to achieve by when.

In the previous table, Juliet and Andy wanted to achieve financial freedom within two years so that they had money to help with their children's education, as well as a legacy to leave behind. Eva and Pete wanted to build their dream retreat business and relocate to warmer climes to enjoy a better quality of life. Both couples were serious about what they wanted to achieve. They decided not to consign their ambitions to the cutting room floor. They wanted to make their dreams a reality, and with a bit of understanding and honest appraisal of what your circumstances are, you can too.

The System's definition of risk

I make no bones about the fact that when you start to scratch the surface of The System you uncover a conundrum that is paradoxical and misleading. Perhaps deliberately so. Or perhaps it just wants us to think that it doesn't serve to look too closely.

Tax rules are labyrinthine. For many people it's easier – and certainly less dull – to take their wage packet each month and allow their employer to deal with their tax codes and their National Insurance payments rather than sitting down to properly work out the tax implications of any investments they might make. The effort to understand how tax works, how it always seems to catch you out anyway, how tax avoidance is frowned upon, despite it not being the same as tax evasion, and how even the highest level politicians can fall foul of its complex rules, is for most people too great an undertaking. If you feel your eyes starting to glaze over whenever anyone attempts to talk to you about tax, it is tempting to push it to one side, ignore it or leave it to someone else to handle. From such a position of wilful ignorance it is just a short step to deciding that anything to do with money making and tax management must be dodgy, if downright too good to be true.

And this gives The System *carte blanche* to exploit our ignorance, whether wilful or innocent, and bamboozle us even more with its own paradoxical and conflicting messages.

In the eyes of The System any investment scheme that is not regulated by the FCA is deemed to be High Risk. This is primarily because individuals investing in regulated schemes have recourse to the financial services compensation model if things go wrong — *unless* of course they have consented to invest in high risk, speculative stocks and shares and signed a paper accepting that they can lose as well as gain capital.

Placing a further burden of risk onto their capital is another feature of the FCA regulated investments — the need to sign a contract granting the investment company permission to skim management fees from their capital, *regardless* of fund returns.

The System will take into account the style of an investment to determine its level of risk. For example, an Individual Savings Account (ISA) is considered a low risk investment providing a fixed defined return over a period of time; but don't get too excited about the return.

Also to be considered is the nature of the organisation or enterprise that is providing the investment. In a nutshell, if they are not FCA registered and cannot offer access to the financial services compensation scheme then they are categorised High Risk.

Where this all gets very misleading and thorny is the fact that there are legions of stories of people who have invested their money in regulated funds only to make no gains, or in the worst case scenario, to lose the lot. My own 'oh shit' moment came about when I realised all the money I'd paid into my pension had not grown at all. My pension investment may have been a low risk thing, but ultimately its lack of growth put my financial future in jeopardy.

So here is the recurring conundrum: if a scheme is being offered by a reputable regulated organisation, then it may be considered low risk. This is despite the fact that the bulk of your money will be invested in the most speculative of products – namely stocks and shares that have no underpinning asset or any capital guarantee. Furthermore, since so many regulated providers do nothing with the value of your money (other than diminish it), they are putting your entire future at risk. It is just as true of the regulated market as it is of Alternatives that when we are trying to determine acceptable levels of risk we need to check whether what we are being offered really exists – or whether all the talk of high risk is little more than an arbitrary smokescreen to play with our emotions and keep us where the System wants us.

Just take a look at how The System categorises investors. High Net Worth individuals have assets of over £250,000 and Sophisticated Investors have demonstrated a high attitude to risk by investing in unregulated markets, unlisted companies and Alternative products.

But it's the ordinary uninitiated investor The System is most concerned with. First of all, there is the underlying tacit implication that the ordinary person on the street is neither intelligent nor capable enough to take control of their own money. This is reinforced by the general reluctance of individuals themselves to take control. Regular investors are referred to as 'retail investors' or 'restricted individuals' and are disallowed by regulation from investing more than ten per cent of their net worth per annum. On the face of it this looks like a sensible step to protect us from our own ignorance and help us safeguard our cash ... until we then understand the risks of heeding the advice of some of the very people whom we are paying to 'protect' us.

The truth is that The System doesn't want us to earn too much money nor ask too many questions. If more of us could make money make money, we would no longer be kept in line by our jobs, and we would no longer be subject to the media messages and propaganda controlled by The System.

Rant over. The fact remains that The System defines risk to suit itself rather than to protect investors. It is far better to take a different view and draw your own conclusions.

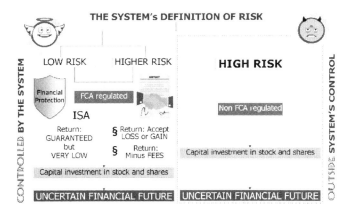

An Alternative definition of risk

In the Alternatives' market, risk is recognised as a relative phenomenon. It is relative to the investor's attitude, position, level of understanding and to the people they are dealing with. While it is prudent to expect that in an unregulated environment there are likely to more bad guys than good guys, it doesn't mean to say that therefore everyone in the unregulated market is trying to run off with your money. The same is true of regulated funds – there are good guys and bad guys in both markets.

So how do you find the good guys?

Whether regulated or unregulated, there are really three approaches:

- trial and error
- due diligence
- referral.

The first of these approaches is the most unfortunate and off-putting, with many people nursing burnt fingers as a result of taking a punt on the wrong thing.

The second is the most sensible. It involves finding out as much about the opportunity as possible, and making sure you are taking on board fact rather than opinion. So much the better if you can meet the individuals behind the opportunity, and if you can see the income generating asset that you are investing in.

The third approach, referrals, can be the most lucrative and successful, as you can be directed straight to the individuals who can make your investment pay. You can reap a much better return than the High Street offers without the regulated middle man who has overheads to meet and commission to earn.

The key point is that investing in Alternatives is all about understanding individuals. First of all, understanding yourself and your own attitude to risk, then understanding the people you are looking to work with. No one can give you advice in this domain. You have to be able to differentiate between fact and opinion and you have to be able to make an informed decision.

When I work with people my only purpose with them is to give them the facts and the right information. It is not about persuasion or selling. They then have to go away and consider their options in the light of their own needs and attitude to risk.

To keep it simple and clear, a *high* risk Alternatives investment is one that displays one or all of the following characteristics:

- no underpinning asset
- no capital guarantee
- no track record of return
- an introducer who's desperate for money and who cannot put your needs ahead of their own.

In contrast, a *low* risk Alternatives Investment has:

- an underpinning asset
- a capital guarantee
- a track record of return
- an introducer who is already making enough from their own investments so they don't actually *need* your business, but *want* to help you.

If you can satisfy all of these criteria and meet the opportunity provider, the chances are you are going to be able to make your money make money. But it's up to you.

Above all, don't be under any illusion that the regulated market never goes near Alternatives. Regulated financial advisors will prevent you from entering the market, but will omit to tell you how the banks and other institutions benefit nightly from trading your deposits on Alternatives and making the big returns that enable them to pay their bonuses, dividends and overheads while we get the bit left over.

Believe me, venturing wide-eyed into Alternatives gives you a window into the world that The System is already using to support itself.

Summary

Determining by when you will achieve financial freedom means:

- Being clear about your resources, timescale and attitude to risk
- Understanding the difference between a high risk and a low risk opportunity
- Taking the time to make informed decisions
- Getting to know the individuals involved in the opportunities you are considering

NOTES

[Page left blank for your reflections]

Where is your money?

It's important to make an honest appraisal of where you keep your money – and also what it's doing for you while it's sitting there. This chapter examines both of these aspects – and recommends what ought to be happening in order to make your money work for you.

The Pots Model

We often refer to wealthy individuals as having pots of money. Conversely we also refer to things on a downward spiral as going to pot. The only question to ask yourself now is which pot usage would you rather choose?

Typically, when something has gone to pot we mean that it is no longer fit for purpose. It's a term that may have come into English usage during the industrial revolution, when defective components on an assembly line were sent back to the smelting pot.

Alternatively, it might have something to do with a different type of pot: Virgin trains have a great information message in their lavatories, warning patrons not to dispose of any unsuitable items in the toilet. As well as the usual nappies and sanitary products the message also excludes items such as 'your ex-boyfriend's sweater' and 'your hopes and dreams'. It is sound, if surprising, advice.

Instead of consigning your financial dreams to the lavatory or the smelting pot, it's time to look for a different set of pots altogether: the pots where you can grow your personal wealth.

I have been using a Pots Model approach to investments for a while now. It's a simple but effective strategy to manage and grow wealth, and I'm going to share it with you here.

The first pot we all have is our current account. This is our bank or building society account that we use day to day to live from.

Our current account pot is typically fed by a generator called a job. This is an *active* generator, since it requires us to do something, namely work, exchanging time for money, in return for financial recompense. Our wage or salary gets paid into our current account pot and is then available to pay our bills and buy our food, clothes, holidays and treats.

Current Account   Job

If we have a good job that pays us a surplus above our daily living expenses, we might sensibly create a second pot, called savings. This may also include our pension, or any capital that we have accumulated through inheritances or house sales or even lottery winnings!

Current Account — Job — Savings

Problems begin if our job doesn't generate enough money to meet our daily living costs. At best we're not able to top up our savings pot. Or we have to pinch from our savings to top up our current account. We might have to find an additional active generator job. At worst, we run up debts on a credit card or through other forms of borrowing.

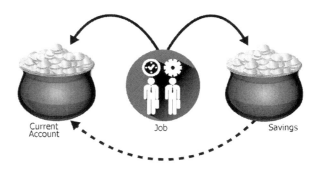

Whichever way, we have less free time, more stress and our capital is reducing. In this situation we are sending the prospect of financial freedom down the pan (or 'to pot'!).

The only way to stem the tide of this all-too-familiar scenario is to divert the leak from savings or debt into a means of generating income without it costing you any more time, effort or stress, and without putting your capital at risk. Protecting your capital at all costs is a mantra that appears often in these pages, and we will talk about it more, later on. Never spend your capital; instead, invest your capital and spend the income. So, rather than eating in to your savings pot to top-up your current account pot, put some of your capital into a scheme that is going to grow your money rather than deplete it. Such schemes are known as *passive* generators.

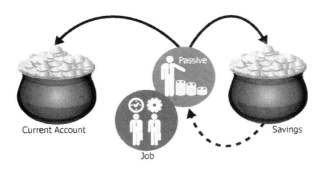

Passive generators create money through the mechanism they use – investment returns, arbitrage, accruals of compound interest, commission payments, sales revenue, royalties – and require no external input from you.

The money created can be used to top up both savings and current account pots, allowing your capital to remain intact.

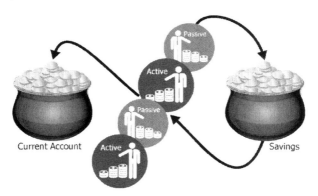

True financial freedom is achieved when *all* of your income is generated from *passive* sources. This is your aim; instead of having to work for money – your money is working for you.

Once you have your pots under control, you will begin to feel quite flush. And your financial dreams will not be heading down the drain.

The compound effect

Whatever pot you put your money in, you need to know how it is being affected by compounding.

It doesn't really matter whether it was Albert Einstein, Benjamin Franklin or John Maynard Keynes who dubbed the compound effect as the Eighth Wonder of the World. (Google it and you'll find numerous references to it by some of the greatest minds.) What is true is that Einstein did describe it as the greatest mathematical discovery of all time. What is also true is that if you learn about its power it could make you rather wealthy. In Douglas Adams' brilliant *Hitchhiker's Guide to the Galaxy* trilogy, the compound interest accrued on a penny deposit you make in any bank on Earth will be enough to pay the bill at Milliways – the Restaurant at the End of the Universe.

So what is the compound effect – and how can it make you rich?

Look away now if mathematical formulae send you cross-eyed – you can catch up further down where the little smiley face is sitting at the beginning of the line. But persevere if you'd like to experience the jaw-dropping awesomeness of converting a penny into over £10.5 million in one single month.

In its simplest mathematical form, the compound effect looks like this:

$$FV = P \times (1 + i)^t$$

Where:

FV = Future Value

P = Principal amount invested

i = interest rate for a given period as a decimal, i.e. 100% = 1.0, 5% = 0.05

t = number of time periods.

In the story of the penny that doubled its value every day during the month of June, the equation would look like this:

$$FV = 0.01 \times (1 + 1.0)^{30}$$

And the incredible FV resulting from this would be £10,737,418.24.

NB To boggle the mind a little bit more, if the month was July and the capital had a further day to compound, the final value would be an astonishing £21,474,836.48!

☺ The important principle involved in compounding is the fact that interest is earned not only on the initial deposit itself, but also on the interest earned from the initial deposit where this is reinvested.

Where an initial deposit of £30,000 is made into a twelve year scheme at an annual interest rate of seven per cent, the following yield pattern is established:

In the first year £30,000 generates £2100 in interest at seven per cent. This then makes the second year's principal amount £32,100, yielding a further £2247 of interest. Where the first year's interest is reinvested in the second year it earns a bonus £147, and where the second year's interest is reinvested in the third year it earns a bonus £157.29 and so on. Each year the interest earned on the previous year's reinvested interest represents bonus 'money for free' growth.

Mathematically put this would be: $FV = 30,000 \times (1 + 0.07)^{12}$

(Sorry – but we've got to try and appreciate the greatness that Einstein raved about.)

At the end of the twelve year term you will have a total pot worth £67,565.75. This is made up of your original capital – £30,000 – and your return of £37,565.75, giving the total of £67,565.75. (Your return is the total figure less the capital you put in.)

A simpler way to think of this, without the need for a scientific calculator, is to use the Rule of 72. By dividing 72 by the interest percentage per period you obtain an approximate number of periods required to double your money.

For example:

> Two per cent per annum doubles in value in approximately 36 years
>
> Five per cent per month doubles in value in approximately 14 months

So what's the best way to take advantage of the compound effect?

First of all, it's best to accept that compounding is not a get rich quick scheme. The compound effect only works over time, and through consistent reinvesting. If you take out some or all of the interest earned as income you drastically diminish the potential returns to be made.

The compound effect works like the victorious tortoise in Aesop's fable: slow and steady wins the race.

If you double the number one, sixty-four times what number will you get?

Or imagine placing a grain of sand on the first square of a chess board, then double the quantity of sand you place square by square until you get to the final square. How many grains of sand will you have?

On the first line of squares you will have accumulated 128 grains of sand. At this point you might be wondering what the big deal is. What's so amazing about 128 grains of sand?

This is the trap our mind has us fall into. Already our mind thinks it has the measure of the situation. It can see 128 grains of sand. It cannot imagine more than what it sees. Like the toddler who can see the finish line, so thinks they've already crossed it when there are still 30 yards to go.

Yet the compound effect is busy at work. Doubling and doubling and doubling the amount of sand on each square all the way down and across the remaining squares.

By the end of the exercise, once the final square has been reached, the number of grains of sand will be 10^{18}. Or in old money:

18,446,744,073,709,551,615.

And if you're wondering how to say it:

Eighteen quintillion, four hundred and forty-six thousand seven hundred and forty-four trillion, seventy-three billion, seven hundred and nine million five hundred and fifty-one thousand, six hundred and fifteen.

I think.

In total this number of grains of sand will weigh 79.2 trillion tonnes. This is equivalent to slightly less than half of the total sand in the 3.5 million square miles of the Sahara Desert. On a chessboard.

How's that for slow and steady accumulation at a stable rate of growth, delivering a number that is almost indefinable? Considering that there are on average 100 billion cells in a human brain, and between 100 and 400 billion stars in the Milky Way, the compounded amount of sand is huge!

The main point is that what you start off with isn't that much, but with repeated action over time what you finish with is unimaginable. It's where mathematics beats the brain.

The compound effect doesn't just apply to numbers and money. It pretty much applies to any amount of effort to achieve any type of goal. Even the effort of thinking. If you spend long enough fearing the worst possible outcome, over time you are more likely to experience the worst possible outcome. Whereas, if you keep your mindset positive, curious and open, then over time you are likely to create better circumstances for yourself.

If you sustain your efforts to work out regularly, the more you do the fitter you become. The fitter you become the smoother and longer your exercise routine. The smoother your routine the quicker you achieve your targets.

Finally, a writer sustaining their daily efforts to write a novel will over time complete the story. The further on they get, the more compelled they are to finish.

So don't give up. Your greatest, quickest gains will occur towards the end of your process. Keep going in order to reap the real rewards of the compound effect.

In contrast, it is also possible to compound your error. Imagine you set sail on a course just one degree off your target direction. For every sixty miles you travel on that course you will deviate a mile off track. So by the time you have covered 840 miles at sea level you will be fourteen miles adrift of your intended destination. Where you want to go will be just on or just under the horizon. So you won't see it.

This is an example of compounding at work to make you miss your target.

Summary

Putting your money to work in the right places means:

- Distinguishing between your different pots
- Protecting your savings capital at all costs
- Understanding how compounding works – and allowing it to work!

NOTES

[Page blank for your reflections]

Who can you rely on?

Understanding the nature of the prevalent financial system in operation around us is an important aspect of our financial education. It helps us to put things in context, decide on our course of action, and make the correct choices to protect our wealth. It also informs us about the people who are best qualified to support us on our journey.

All systems rely on inputs in order to generate their required output. Your car needs fuel to get you from A to B. Your body is a system that relies on a complex mix of food, oxygen, water and love to power an active, engaged and productive person.

Likewise, financial systems the world over rely on the input of cash, in the shape of taxes and levies, in order to support government, infrastructure and a stable society. Our financial System also needs to secure its place as a cog in the wheels of other systems, such as the EU and the IMF.

In order to navigate The System, you would be wise to look for someone to help you. As an uninitiated person, who nevertheless is curious and hungry for a better financial future, you may immediately assume that the best people to consult would be in the professional sector.

It can be a scary step to take, so it's natural to look for help and advice from qualified people.

Professional advice

If you have questions about investments or pensions, you might immediately think of talking to an Independent Financial Advisor (IFA). If you run a business and want some financial insight, you might call your accountant for a chat. If you are approaching later life and are concerned about your financial legacy, you might consider a conversation with a tax advisor. Or if you are looking to radically change your life circumstances, such as getting a divorce, you would most likely approach a lawyer. Then, when the financial stress bites, you may need a prescription from a medic to see you through ...

Each of the professionals listed above have their role to play in giving you access to some small element of The System, or at least applying a sticking plaster when the ravages of it all get too much.

What's important to be aware of, however, is the context within which each of the professionals operates, and their individual entanglement with The System.

Independent Financial Advisors are a case in point. This is where the world of illusion meets that of investment finance. According to the dictionary definition, IFAs in the UK are 'professionals who offer independent advice on financial matters to their clients, and recommend suitable financial products from the whole of the market'.

'Whole of market' is a curious phrase. On the face of it, it would suggest that IFAs are qualified to advise on a vast array of investment products and strategies that represent pretty much anything and everything investible in the UK at any given moment. It's a phrase that promises a lot of knowledge and expertise, and is intended to make you feel like you are receiving the most comprehensive guidance available.

However, 'whole of market' is a very specific term that has been coined to reflect a UK regulatory position. In fact, 'whole of market' refers only to those financial products that are covered by the Financial Markets Act 2000, which is the key regulatory legislation policed by the FCA, and which represents only a fraction of the real market.

Similarly, the word 'independent' is a bit of a misnomer. Independence is a term used to reassure consumers that their go-to financial professional is not being manipulated by any particular profit-making institution.

The fact is that in order to practise as an IFA an individual is required to pay a professional membership fee to the FCA, and is only allowed to advise on those products that the Authority has identified within its regulatory jurisdiction, misleadingly titled 'whole of market'.

So is your IFA really independent? Perhaps in the sense that they set their own fees and are not in the pay of any particular financial profit-making institution – although even that is a moot point for many advisors you'll find, who work as affiliates to large investment banks and houses, and have so-called privileged access to the specific trusts, schemes and products that those institutions offer, usually with a high ticket management fee.

The important thing to keep in mind is that IFAs and the FCA operate within a closed system, with a purposefully narrow scope that keeps consumers on the less enlightened side of the truth. This is The System at work. It offers investors a smaller range of opportunities to choose from than is truly available, and makes the whole thing seem extremely daunting, complicated and risky, so that you find solace in the arms of the experts and continue working in your job, paying your taxes and the management fees of your investment portfolio. When you add to this the charade of regulatory tension that is expected of any Authority organisation, seemingly adding more and more hoops for its subjects to jump through – to the extent that the IFAs complain about how difficult the FCA makes their business – this is testament to how much care they must be taking with your money.

Another illusory factor in the equation is that of the risk profile of the population. IFAs pay indemnity insurance to cover themselves in the case of client demands for financial compensation. However, the range of client risk profiling is highly controlled, such that IFAs encourage less risk aversion in their clients to minimise their indemnity premium. So if the whole of the financial industry seems to be walking around talking about not touching high risk investments with a barge pole, it is helpful to know that it is because if they did their insurance overheads would go sky-high. Not a good position for a small business. As a result, we each have our attitude to risk artificially managed on our behalf to suit the pocket of the financial advice profession.

The bottom line is it serves The System to keep you ignorant – ignorant of whole of market, ignorant of the payable fees, ignorant of your own attitude to risk. So it is not surprising that you can go through life completely unaware of the opportunities you might be missing out on, all the while paying through the nose and being told by others seemingly better qualified than you what you should think.

Is this an acceptable deal?

Friends and family

Perhaps with these thoughts in mind you would prefer to rely on the people in your life whom you do actually trust, such as your family and friends. Surely they wouldn't try and dupe you?

Unless your family and friends have themselves got a proven track record of breaking out of the rat race and investing successfully, it is highly unlikely their level of financial education is any better than your own. Listening to their advice is far more likely to keep you stuck doing the same thing you've always done, playing it safe, and certainly not chasing a dream that would ultimately take you away from their bosom.

Similarly, you wouldn't take seriously the insights of the know-it-all who sits in the pub all day. While it serves you to be circumspect about the motivation and interests of financial professionals within The System, you must also be careful to establish how much experience and success people around you have achieved. And certainly be aware of how much beer has been sunk prior to any helpful advice being doled out.

Stephen Hawking said: 'The greatest enemy of knowledge is not ignorance, it is the illusion of knowledge.'

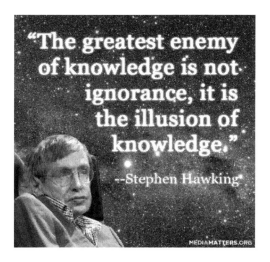

How right he is, especially in the realm of finance and personal wealth.

Sometimes the ego can trick us into believing we are experts in a subject when we have developed an awareness of only one tiny aspect of it. With regards to our finances it can get us into extremely hot water. Or it can cause us to miss opportunities.

On the other hand, real knowledge sets us free. It gives us understanding and increases our choices, especially when it is sought out of genuine curiosity and a desire for self-improvement.

However, there are a number of factors which keep us from real knowledge, and which trap us in an illusory world. Here are the five things to look out for in ourselves and others:

1. Lack of financial education

First of all, we need to know what we don't know. Or rather we need to accept that our financial education is generally woeful and that there is a load of stuff to learn about and understand. There is no shame in ignorance – acknowledging this provides the perfect starting point.

Amongst other things we need to appreciate: the power of compounding; the importance of due diligence; the difference between regulated investments and the Alternatives' market; the benefits of leverage; what differentiates an asset from a liability; how to protect our capital at all costs; and what opportunities there are to make money make money.

Check in with yourself as you read that paragraph. Do you clearly understand all the terminology? Hand on heart? If that question is making you uncomfortable there could be a big gap between what you think you know and what you actually know – a simple case of illusion vs reality.

If any of these topics is making you draw a blank, then do not worry. All you are lacking is financial education and this book is designed to help rectify that.

2.   Lack of curiosity

At a certain point in our life we stop being curious. We are told as children that curiosity killed the cat and are subsequently paralysed by our inability to ask questions. Maybe we are afraid of looking stupid. Maybe our parents and teachers made us shy about asking too many questions when we were children. Or maybe we just do not know which questions to ask.

The simple law of cause and effect dictates that if you don't ask you don't get. Knowledge cannot be decanted into a mind that isn't curious or interested. So it pays to build your curiosity muscle and develop the skill of asking questions; otherwise, you run the risk of being forever fed a diet of illusory knowledge that doesn't serve your dreams and goals.

3. Our fearful ego

Knowledge is power, so the story goes. Perhaps this is why our ego is so quick to claim knowledge, even the illusion of it, because it bolsters our primeval sense of superiority.

You may have met the know-it-all character who sits in the pub every day nursing a lukewarm pint. He (and yes I'm afraid it usually is a bloke) reads a bit of the paper, reminisces about his days in business, has dabbled in stocks, but these days is more likely to come up with racing tips. And just because he's handy with cryptic crosswords and pub quizzes people think he's a genius. In his narrow universe people gravitate towards him as the oracle, the person who would be 'in the know' about stuff, and they seek his advice. His ego rises to it, he feels duty bound to expound to his audience, and suddenly he is kidding not only his buddies but also himself that he is the one to ask.

Know-it-alls stop asking questions. They stop being curious. They live in a rigid world of illusory 'facts' that they have persuaded themselves are the whole truth. When we live this way we become afraid of anything that challenges our preconceived ideas and beliefs. Then fear paralyses us further, and causes us to become more entrenched in the comfort of our illusions.

Beware the influence of your fearful ego in your quest for knowledge!

4. Misinformation

Also beware the limited knowledge of others who purport to know what they're talking about. The chap in the pub is one thing, but a whole barrage of influential journalists, writers, television and radio anchors are opinion formers in their own right, and know it.

Maddeningly, much that we read and hear in the financial press and on the media comes from a misinformed position. It seeks to manipulate us, pandering to the illusion of knowledge and using our ignorance as fodder.

Sensationalist headlines reel us in to articles that often serve to reinforce our fears about scams, or our cultural conditioning about the moral dubiousness of money. When the BBC tried to whip up a storm about the then Prime Minister David Cameron's off-shore investments, the tax expert it chose to interview very calmly asserted that a more representative, but clearly less interesting, headline would be 'Man makes off-shore investment and declares it on his tax return.'

For many of us what we read and see in the media has the power to put us off the scent of our own curiosity. It encourages us back into our illusory knowledge boxes, where we feel most comfortable, and where we can be more easily controlled and duped by a financial System which needs us to toe the line, work our jobs, spend our money and pay our taxes.

Don't be hoodwinked by the manipulative tendencies of the media. Keep being curious and asking questions that lead to truth rather than illusion.

5. Our cultural conditioning

Received wisdom and illusory knowledge can become one and the same thing. Beliefs about wealth and personal finance are handed down generationally, and rarely does anyone ask the really disruptive questions that lead to real knowledge.

Professional opinion can also fall foul of this, as anyone operating in the financial industry will testify. The prohibition of any investment advice that is not regulated by the FCA lends weight to the myth that Alternatives are inherently risky, which then reinforces the illusory perception of risk in the minds of prospective investors.

On and on spins the wheel of our conditioning – until someone jams a spanner in the works. Could that someone be you?

Wealth gurus

Of course there are self-proclaimed wealth gurus operating on the Internet. They promise to unlock your wealth potential, teach you all the secrets of a wealthy mindset, and help you along the way to becoming the millionaire you always dreamed you could be.

In a lot of cases they are credible business owners in their own right who have made millions, and who now choose to share their knowledge and methodology with aspiring investors. They make huge amounts of training material available, much of which is worthwhile and useful, and may even host group coaching calls to guide people through their programmes.

Fundamentally, however, they are continually attempting to upsell their intellectual property and reel people in to ever more costly educational experiences. Again, be circumspect about who you pay your money to in this regard. Financial education needn't cost a lot, and certainly paying coaching fees will not guarantee to make you wealthy.

So, if not an IFA, nor the beer-soaked wise guy down the pub, nor an online wealth guru, nor yet the tarot card reader – who can you approach to help you along in your journey to financial freedom? And how do you identify a good candidate?

Experienced individuals

Ideally, you are looking to find people who are on the same journey to financial freedom as you are. There are growing numbers of networking groups where people are trying to get out of the rat race, and who are focusing on achieving their own financial freedom dream. Many of these groups in the UK are currently aligned with property investment; however, you may also find network marketing groups and groups of people interested in growing passive or residual income.

There are also many business networking groups in the UK; but these do tend to attract solopreneur businesses run by people who are selling their hours, and exchanging their time for money, rather than people who are trying to grow their passive income. Network marketing professionals sometimes frequent these types of meetings – if you're interested in finding out about residual income opportunities, these people are good contacts to make, and could potentially lead you into a different network.

Once you have connected with like-minded people who share an intention, either implicitly or explicitly, to break out of the rat race, the next thing to look for is a mentor.

A mentor is an experienced, successful person who is willing to give you their time to answer your questions and guide you as you make your first steps on the road to financial freedom. They are likely to be an open, approachable person, who has consciously chosen to share their experience of financial freedom in order to help others on their journey.

The role of a mentor is to listen and to give you information and suggestions, but ultimately to let you make your own informed decisions. A very experienced individual will have a broad range of knowledge about the different options that may be available to you, and will be able to offer you soft advice about different opportunities and approaches.

Think for a moment about the person you are yourself becoming as you achieve your independence. Would you like to become a flash extrovert, flaunting your cash but caring very little about the others around you? Or would you like to become a more understated but nonetheless confident and friendly individual who is more than willing to guide others along a similar path? Think about who you would like to meet – and look for the qualities you are developing in yourself.

Although your mentor can give you suggestions about how you might proceed, there are three key pieces of information that you must determine for yourself.

These are: your resources and capital; your investment timescale; and your attitude to risk.

In order to determine the first piece of information, work through or revisit the financial planner template in Section Two. Then reflect on where you want to get to and by when – this will determine your timescale. To understand your attitude to risk, be sure to read to the end of the book. If you feel excited and motivated by the end, your attitude to risk may be relatively high. If you can't stomach the rest of the book, you'll know you're pretty risk averse, and so perhaps this isn't the route for you!

Another key thing to determine about your prospective mentor is what their motive is for working with you. In my case I created the My Goal Is business in order to pass on my knowledge and experiences of moving away from traditional investment strategies and creating wealth through asset backed Alternative Investments. It costs my clients nothing to work with me. If they invest in any of the schemes I introduce, I get paid an introducer's fee, and in some cases I receive residual income based on their investment too.

I can work with people to develop strategies that suit their needs, depending on the amount they have to invest, over what timescale, and how aggressively. But ultimately it's no skin off my nose if people decide it isn't for them. I never push my clients.

Fortunately, I've got myself into a position where I would like to have your business, for your sake, but I don't need your business for my own sake.

Protect your capital at all costs

Wherever your capital comes from – a windfall, an inheritance, a remortgage or a pension fund – the first thing you might think of doing with it is what? Spend it? Grow it? Or gamble it?

For many people spending their capital is the default position. They may decide to treat themselves to a few of life's luxuries, or they may need to release their capital as living expenses.

For the uninitiated they may think about trying to double their money by backing the favourite at the races. Or taking a trip to the casino to see how much they can make on the tables. Obviously these are not safe bets at all, and there is far more chance of blowing your money than growing your money in these scenarios.

More sensible would be to invest your capital in a safe scheme and ideally take the interest as income while your pot remains ring-fenced and intact.

While some eccentric individuals might choose to hoard their money under the mattress, the majority of people choose to keep their capital in a bank. Each person's money up to the value of £75,000 is protected – meaning that should there be another run on the banks ahead of a crash, everyone's capital up to this amount is safe and recoverable. So if you have savings up to this capital amount safely stashed in a bank account you should be OK.

Protecting your capital is not always about others making off with your money. You must also protect your capital from yourself. No matter how you make your main income, be sure that you are living within your means and are able to periodically add to your savings capital. If you begin to get into debt you will have to break into your savings pot to cover your repayments – thus depleting your own capital. Better to be aware of your income and essential outgoings, and to develop your ability to budget effectively and manage your net cash flow to avoid having to eat into your savings (or even have to borrow) whenever you go into debt.

As for your ability to live off the interest that your capital generates – well that's another matter entirely. Let's just say at this point that it is unlikely with High Street interest rates that you can sack the boss and live off the cream of your capital.

For this to become a reality you will have to look to more sophisticated financial mechanisms that make better returns – at least to bump your passive income up to hundreds of pounds rather than hundreds of pence.

But of course this will also require you to shift your capital out of the relatively safe, albeit nonproductive, haven of the bank or pension fund into a scheme that demands a more active role for your money.

Whatever scheme you identify the main thing to ensure is that your capital is not at risk. The problem with a lot of managed funds is that the fees due are taken from your capital as opposed to the profits of your investment. Over time this eats away your cash, leaving you with a depleted fund making even lower returns.

Protecting your capital at all costs means avoiding schemes that nibble away at your deposit. Make sure the management fees payable are taken from the investment profits rather than your capital.

In the Alternatives' world the fundamental approaches to protecting your capital are to conduct thorough due diligence on all investment opportunities, and to ensure you either have a capital guarantee or first charge on a fixed asset.

A capital guarantee means that your deposit is recoverable in its entirety from the scheme regardless of the trading success of the fund.

Securing your capital on a fixed asset is exactly what the banks and lenders do when they loan you money through a mortgage. They effectively take ownership of the property – and should you default on the payments they can repossess the property and sell it in order to recover their capital.

The same principle can be applied when you invest in opportunities that involve a fixed asset. You can protect your capital by ensuring you can reclaim it through the sale of the asset, should the venture fail.

Understanding how your chosen investment opportunity will support you in protecting your capital is a crucial part of your due diligence process. The next section looks in more detail at what due diligence is, and how to conduct it.

Due diligence

Depending on your attitude to risk, and the risk profile of the investment opportunity you are considering, it is nevertheless always vital to conduct your own process of investigation in order to put your mind at rest that you are not just playing poker with your capital.

It took me a while to work out how to do the due diligence on Alternative Investments. The returns being offered put High Street rates into the shade. Most people I met who offered Alternative

Investments seemed honest and plausible. The material they gave me was well presented. They all had great testimonials. But was it all true?

In the end I came up with a four step process that I still work with to this day. Here's what I do:

Step 1 – does it make sense?

What I'm looking for here is sufficient information from the provider to help me to see how it all works. I want to get enough information that would enable me to replicate the opportunity if I so choose (I'm not going to). This is all about openness, honesty and trust. If they won't give me this information, then I don't proceed.

A key piece of information is the exit strategy. If the investment has to be sold to someone else in order to get your money out, make sure that there is a proven, established resale market. If it relies on a market that may or may not exist, steer well clear!

Key questions to ask:

>Q1 Whose idea was it and how does it work?

>Q2 By when can you send me an information pack?

>Q3 How do I get my money back out?

Step 2 – return vs risk

When you explore Alternative Investments, many of the returns being offered are way above anything available in the High Street or traditional regulated investments.

The standard mantra you hear is 'Higher returns means high risk!' But is this true?

I see Alternative Investments falling into two categories – asset backed and speculative (non-asset backed).

Asset backed opportunities typically invest your funds on a group basis as a first charge against an underpinning asset – a building, a piece of land etc. The value of the loan against the value of the underpinning assets is important here. Complete Step 1 and then make sure the value of the underpinning assets is stated. Returns in excess of twenty per cent per annum are perfectly possible from these opportunities with little or no risk. This type of opportunity is in many cases also acceptable for pension funds to invest into.

Speculative opportunities are exactly what they say – speculative. Usually involving trading in some form, your money is secured against nothing. There is no underpinning asset to make a charge against. Step 1 of the due diligence process is really important now, as are Steps 3 and 4.

Investing in speculative opportunities does require you to take a deep breath and a leap of faith. The trick here is to dip your toe in the water first. Make a deposit, check out the results, take money out, pay back in and see if it performs as you've been told it performs.

And no matter how good the returns are, you never, ever, put all of your money in speculative opportunities! Just bear in mind that you *could* lose your money.

Returns of between two and five per cent per month are perfectly possible. I currently receive around 5.1 per cent per month tax-free on some of my funds and five per cent per month gross of tax on other funds. (Yes, that is *per month*.)

Key questions:

> Q4 What's the value of the underpinning asset?
>
> Q5 How does the charge/capital guarantee work?
>
> Q6 What's the minimum investment?
>
> Q7 By when will I see the results?

Step 3 – physically put your hands on it!

You can do this in many ways. If you're investing in land or buildings etc, go and visit it. Make sure it exists. I went out to Leipzig to look at an investment opportunity. Ryan Air flights are very cheap!

You should also meet face to face with the people behind the opportunity. Look them in the eye and get them to tell you about the opportunity. Get their email address and mobile phone number. This approach precludes you from most corporate investments – they won't give you their email address or their mobile phone numbers!

Small, niche providers are where you will end up. You become part of the 'family' and you get passed information that can lead to other good investment opportunities.

Key questions:

> Q8 Where is the asset and when can I visit?
>
> Q9 Who's behind the opportunity and when can I meet them?
>
> Q10 What's the email address and the mobile phone number of the opportunity provider?

Step 4 – never be first in!

Social proof is important. If you are first in there will be none – everyone else will be waiting for you to report *your* experience!

Google everything. But remember that there is a load of rubbish, opinion, bias, spite, retaliation etc in the stuff you will read. Sorting out the facts and reality will not be easy.

So, talk to other investors. What are their experiences?

No due diligence process is fool proof. I've made mistakes. But I've minimised them. Spread your risk by investing in Alternatives involving different asset classes:

- property
- businesses
- equities
- commodities

and you won't go far wrong.

Key questions:

> Q11 Who else has invested and when can I speak with them?
>
> Q12 What are the experiences of other investors and how can I find these out?

> Q13 What information is available on the Internet about the opportunity?

Remember that taking control of your financial freedom provides no quick fix solution. You still have to do your homework, talk to people and listen to others' experiences.

Other important questions to bear in mind are:

> Q14 Who gets rich from the deal?
>
> Q15 Who's getting the lion's share of the money?
>
> Q16 Where is the provider/introducer being paid from – your capital or the profits of the investment?

After my own 'oh shit' moment, I started to collect a lot of information. Loads of stuff didn't make sense and out of maybe seventy plus opportunities that I looked into there remain only six or seven that I still work with regularly.

It's important to recognise that just because you are making money doesn't make you a level-headed human being. In fact, it could be destabilising. Make sure you have gathered a Power Team of advisors around you, such as a mortgage broker, a tax advisor, an accountant and a mentor. These need to be people you both like and trust.

And crucially, no matter how attractive an opportunity appears, you must know when it's best to walk away.

Summary

Knowing who you can rely on means:

- Being confident in yourself to protect your capital and conduct due diligence
- Being clear on the motives and limitations of all those you might consider approaching for help
- Understanding all the factors influencing would-be advisors
- Asking the right questions
- Seeking out experienced, like-minded mentors

NOTES

[Page left blank for your reflections]

EPILOGUE TO SECTION ONE

If you're still reading this far it's good to have you with us.

Having completed Section One you now know something of the principles involved in achieving financial freedom. And you know how to distinguish illusion from reality. You also know why we tend to delude ourselves – and how to weed out those who are trying to dupe us.

I hope you have developed a new perspective on The System and what it offers. Mainly, I hope that you have resolved to take less at face value, and to ask more questions about the received wisdom of getting a job and trusting that your pension/savings are going to see you through, just because they are wrapped up in a glossy-looking fund management product.

From this point on you get to apply what you are learning to your own financial reality. And, just like the laws of compounding, your biggest results won't manifest until you reach the end of the process – so don't give up. Keep reading. Keep learning. Keep enquiring.

Enjoy the next steps in the journey.

SECTION TWO

–

Your Financial Freedom Journey Starts Here

6

Start your journey

Now that you have begun to learn about the financial realities of The System, and a little about the important mechanisms and tactics that you must deploy in order to break free of it, it's time for you to address your own financial reality, and determine the steps you need to take next on your journey to financial freedom.

What you have to do to promote your own financial freedom may not be the same as anyone else. You have your own unique starting point and set of motivations. You have your own dreams to fulfil and your own vision to achieve. No one else can dictate these things for you. You have to discover them for yourself, and then take the appropriate steps to move you closer to where you wish to be.

For that reason, this section of the book aims to help you focus on your own situation. This is where you get to confront your own financial reality, and put plans in place to set yourself free from the rat race, from exchanging your time for money, from the constraints of high street returns and, most importantly, from ignorance to understanding.

Once again I'm following the model of the Six Honest Serving Men as I encourage you to explore the Why, When, What, How, Who and Where of your financial future.

There are questions to reflect on, and templates to fill out. There are stories to read about others' experiences, and references to follow. This is where you can put what you are learning into the context of your own situation. This is when things can get really exciting – when you begin to realise that what you are learning needn't just be a nice-to-know theory, but that there is a real possibility of applying it to improve your own circumstances.

Prepare to be motivated! Financial freedom is already within your grasp.

7

What's your story?

To get yourself focused on your own situation, it's time to reflect on your experiences so far. Before diving in to the questions that follow, go back to the Introduction and cast your eye over my career timeline.

Reflective questions

- Spend a moment bringing to mind the milestones and way-markers of your own journey, then make a timeline of the significant moments/employment/transitions in your life so far.
- What are your assumptions about money?
- What have you learned about money from your parents/schooling/peer group?
- How well do you feel you understand money?
- On your timeline, map out your periods of security, independence and freedom according to the definitions I gave in Section One. By when do you wish to become financially free?
- How would you describe your situation now – secure, independent or free?

- Describe your 'oh shit' moment, assuming you've already had it. If not, when is it likely to happen? (Of course, if you want to avoid that moment altogether, read on!)
- Use the next two blank pages for your notes. Throughout this book we've left additional blank pages for you to record your thoughts and the answers to the questions posed in the text. You may find it beneficial to keep a separate financial freedom journal and record your responses in there.

NOTES

[Page left blank for your reflections]

NOTES

[Page left blank for your reflections]

8

Motivation: Why do you want to be financially free?

There are lots of personal development books and gurus and courses, offering everything from practical insight to spiritual guidance. And while I am far from a New Age enthusiast I do find that most of us are searching for the same thing in different guises – peace of mind.

Working towards your financial freedom could look like material obsession. Lots of people dream of winning the lottery and imagine how it would change their lives, how differently they would live. They'd be able to go on expensive holidays, drive flash cars, live in the home of their dreams, give up work forever.

But one thing that we overlook when it comes to day-dreaming about our ideal, wealthy existence is this: what really makes us happy.

And it's worth understanding what makes us happy right now, ahead of attaining our financial goal, because we are sadly mistaken if we think that having more money to spend will do it.

It's true that having no money worries definitely helps in terms of delivering peace of mind. But on top of that how do we live? What makes a peaceful, worry-free life worth living? This is where our happiness lies.

The importance of happiness

As you approach the question of what makes you happy, it's vital that you are honest with yourself. One of my clients (who wishes to remain anonymous) made the mistake of not fully confronting his circumstances during the process of setting his financial goals, and ended up with the wrong plan in place.

When I first met him at a property investors' networking meeting he was doing a back-breaking sales job, involving thousands of motorway miles and crippling hours behind the wheel.

He was making no secret of the fact that he was keen to escape the particular bit of the rat race that he found himself in. Despite being a young man in his early forties, his health was suffering and he was desperate to do something different.

We had a few further meetings to go through his plan and explore some of the opportunities that were available to him, and eighteen months after our initial contact my client was in a position to 'sack the boss'.

Taking up the story he said:

> 'I had to give three months' notice but I was officially on paid gardening leave before I had to hand over my company car. During that time I wouldn't be exaggerating if I said that life seemed like a party. I wasn't being held accountable to anyone, I still had certain perks of my job, was still earning, but was also making enough passive income to cover all my expenses.
>
> 'I felt like a different life was there for the taking. The trouble is I wasn't being entirely honest with myself about how different that life needed to be.'

Very soon the whole dream began to unravel. My client realised that he didn't just require to do something different career wise, he also wanted to make significant changes in his life overall that he hadn't budgeted for.

> 'I realise that when I first started planning to leave my job, I thought that was all I needed to change in my life. Very quickly though it became apparent that it wasn't all about the job.

> 'I can see now that there were issues which I just kept pushing back and not facing up to – and unfortunately twelve months after sacking the boss the choices I initially made have proved inadequate to my new needs.'

My client's journey to financial freedom has suffered from a rather existential problem – namely the discovery that while he thought he was a certain person with certain goals and ambitions, it turns out that he is actually rather different from who he originally thought he was.

> 'Life circumstances change. When I first spoke to Neil about financial freedom I had a particular plan in mind. But over time my circumstances have changed in a way that the original plan is no longer tenable.
>
> 'If I were to do it differently I would have come up with separate plans to cater for different life scenarios, not just financial.
>
> 'If your circumstances change it's crucial you have a plan B to fall back on and you shouldn't risk being out of pocket.'

My client also learned that it serves not to be too hasty.

> 'The old adage "don't put all your eggs in one basket" is very true. It can be tempting to

take the easiest income generating option but you have to protect your capital and don't tie it all up in the same scheme. Not only does this safeguard against a scheme failing or becoming unavailable, it also gives you more flexibility should your needs change.'

Unfortunately for my client his experience demonstrates the importance of honesty and patience in making your financial plans in order to avoid costly choices. Happily though, he had protected his capital at all costs and was able to develop and implement Plan B.

Reflective questions

- What does financial freedom mean to you?
- What makes you happy?
- What do you really want – for yourself, your family, your friends and humanity?
- What is important about it?
- Why is it important to you?
- What will your legacy be?

NOTES

[Page left blank for your reflections]

When the hard work pays off

It is important to know what you want to achieve. This gives you impetus. It is highly motivating to know that you are going to be able to do whatever makes you happy whenever you want to do it.

My wife Christine and I love to travel. Last summer we spent three consecutive weeks touring Europe in our motorhome. We took in some sights that reminded us of our childhood, and visited some places that our own children have been to and only told us about. As a result, we travelled through Belgium, Germany, Austria, Switzerland and Italy. We experienced the sadness of the Great War cemeteries, the majesty of the mountains, the charm of Venetian piazzas and the splendour of sunsets over Lake Garda. It was a truly fabulous trip.

The decision to cut loose for that long was not one we took lightly. We've never had the opportunity to do it before, prevented either by our jobs or a lack of funds. But last year it became a real possibility for us simply because we are approaching the pinnacle of financial independence.

We're no longer reliant on anyone else's rules about how long our holiday can be, and we suffer no financial penalty for taking as much time off as we like. (And with diesel at 90p a litre on the Continent the cost of travel was kept within reasonable limits too!)

In other words, our income didn't suffer because we weren't in the office. Our business concerns and our investments produce enough money to keep things ticking over while we enjoy precious recreation together. In 2016 we managed to get away for four consecutive weeks, and for 2017 we've already booked our five week trip of a lifetime to Australia.

In this section I'm encouraging you to think carefully about your motivation to become financially free. Why do you want it? What will your life be like once you have achieved it? And do you have the staying power to make it?

We know that our goals are worth achieving when we can visualise what life will be like for us when we have put in the hard work to get there. And it is hard work. If material gain is really all you're interested in, then it is unlikely you will stay the distance. Material gain is an enabler, nothing else. You will have a better chance of achieving your dreams if you are crystal clear about what money will enable you to do. You need to come to this quest with far more robust intentions than 'making a lot of dosh' – and you need a strategy to fall back on when the going gets tough.

Reflective questions

- How strong is your motivation to achieve it?
- From what you currently know, what will it take you to achieve it?
- Who will help you along the way?
- Who will try to stop you achieving your goal?
- From what you currently know, what are the likely obstacles that will prevent you from achieving it?
- What will you do to keep going when things get tough?
- How does reflecting on your process and potential obstacles affect your level of motivation?

NOTES

[Page left blank for your reflections]

Giving back

For all of my adult life I have been a member of a Round Table or Rotary Club. I've always wanted to help other people, and the Service above Self ethic has played a prominent role in my upbringing. This is something that has always been true for me. Being part of Rotary International, the largest non-governmental service organisation in the world, and being able to give my time and skills for the benefit of others without collecting a pay cheque, has been a constant aspect of my personal life. It makes me happy.

Now that I am approaching financial freedom I am able to do more for the charity. In November 2015 Christine and I had the privilege of sponsoring my Rotary Club's Remembrance Ball, raising funds for Combat Stress, the charity that supports service men and women suffering with Post Traumatic Stress Syndrome. We had a great night, and all the money raised that evening went directly to the beneficiaries.

Money is enabling me to do more and contribute more to causes that have been important to me throughout my adult life. When we create wealth for ourselves we have the ability and the opportunity to help those who are less fortunate than us. This can take many forms, and often it's our time, knowledge and experience that are more valuable than our money.

In my experience my financial freedom journey has taken five years. During that time, I went to some very dark places in my mind. It's not that long ago that we were pretty broke. As I write in early 2016 it's only eighteen months to be exact since we were really struggling. For three and a half years I woke up at night in a cold sweat, with my mind playing games and with an overwhelming feeling of wanting to withdraw. I have no doubt that during the darkest hours I was verging on depression. (Christine had no idea. I shall be explaining it all to her during our long, upcoming flight to Australia for our five week trip of a lifetime. Sorry, sweetheart.)

Eventually, despite the fear, and the temptation to quit and fall back into my old thinking about money, the process began to pay off. Money started to come in. We had held fast and followed our plan and finally we started to see the returns we hoped for. In the end, thanks to the effect of compounding, the step from financial independence to financial freedom is a relatively short one. With compounding the biggest gains happen at the end of the time period. So it pays not to give up, to stay the distance and to stick with the process. Be aware that old thinking and the scare-mongering of propaganda and nay-sayers can still pull you back, especially during the darkest hours. It can be very tempting to give up on your dream – unless of course your dream is very real and vivid and compelling.

What would having enough passive income to clear your debt, cover your costs and support the lifestyle you enjoy enable you to do? Maybe you'd finally get round to writing that novel; or trek the Himalayas; or set up a new educational trust; or sponsor a talented sports team; or create a new business; or pursue your alter ego? The most important thing is that it makes you happy, so that you not only achieve peace of mind but also live a fulfilled life.

What does fulfilment mean to you?

Uh-oh. I mentioned hard work. And fulfilment. Are you sitting there in a quandary about what makes you happy? Maybe you have never really thought about it before. Are you allowing the thought that there is hard work ahead to put you off?

Falling back into the old habits that governed you when you were under the illusion that you needed to keep your job and stay Just Over Broke is the worst thing you can do.

```
                      morality,
                      creativity,
                     spontaneity,
                   problem solving,
                   lack of prejudice,
                   acceptance of facts
Self-actualisation
                   ─────────────────────
                         self-esteem,
                    confidence, achievement,
Esteem             respect of others, respect by others
                   ─────────────────────
Love/Belonging       friendship, family, sexual intimacy
                   ─────────────────────
                   security of body, of employment, of resources,
Safety              of morality, of the family, of health, of property
                   ─────────────────────
Physiological      breathing, food, water, sex, sleep, homeostasis, excretion
```

According to Maslow's Hierarchy, once we have our physiological needs met and once we feel safe and secure, the next thing we look for is love, friendship and belonging. Once we feel like we belong somewhere, we need to garner others' respect and esteem, and finally, once we have gained the confidence to be ourselves and to achieve our goals, we can then realise our true potential. We can self-actualise. This will mean different things to different people. *It's your job to consider what it means to you.* It might mean doing more or doing less: being more or less active, creative or contemplative. Whatever it is, it has to be about you, and the legacy you wish to leave behind.

A lot of people will oscillate within a personal comfort zone, not quite reaching as far as their goal, but just about managing to keep their feet out of the fire of penury. In money terms, the lower echelons of Maslow's Hierarchy correspond to establishing an income, clearing financial debt and achieving financial freedom. Thereafter, love, respect and self-actualisation rely on a different set of drivers than material ones. For myself I'm not looking for adoration or adulation. I'd simply like to be recognised as someone who is pragmatic and talks a lot of sense. I hope you're in agreement so far.

The journey towards financial freedom is as much about your development and behaviour as it is about accumulating wealth. We've all got experience of arrogant wealthy individuals who treat others badly because they feel like the big *I am* flashing the cash. It's one of those things that gives money a bad name, and reinforces the old thinking that money is the root of all evil.

So it's important to think about who you are becoming during your financial journey. What are you learning about yourself and, more importantly, about other people? How are you relating to those around you? What new habits and ways of interacting with others are you looking to form?

One of the great financial gurus of recent years is Tony Robbins. His three step approach to mastering money and being financially successful is: Do more. Give more. Be more valuable than anyone else in your sector.

It is a journey that may take a number of years, but you don't have to wait until your mid-sixties, as I did. You can embark on your journey as soon as tomorrow. Achieving financial freedom begins with choosing to be free. And all journeys have to begin with the first step.

As Mark Twain said, 'The secret to getting ahead is getting started.'

So start right now.

Reflective questions

- What will your legacy be?
- How can you help others?
- What cause would you gladly give your skills and talents to?
- What are you learning about yourself?
- What are you learning about other people?
- How can you be more valuable than anyone else in your sector?
- What kind of person do you aspire to become?

NOTES

[Page left blank for your reflections]

NOTES

[Page left blank for your reflections]

Begin with the end in mind

A few years before my sixtieth birthday I decided I would like to achieve a physical goal before I reached my seventh decade.

Not generally one to do things by halves, I set my sights on the London Marathon.

I trained for a year and got ready to run. Then shortly before the Big Day I came down with a virus. I had to withdraw. I was gutted.

So I entered the following year. My training programme was progressing OK until suddenly I got a searing pain in one of my knees. I couldn't run any more. I was in agony. The consultant at the hospital informed me that I'd worn a hole in the cartilage behind my kneecap.

'You can forget running,' he said. 'Get a bike.'

So I did. And it sat in my garage for months, until one sunny day, when we had a family barbecue.

I may have had one or two beers at this point, but not long into our meal I heard myself saying, 'I'm going to cycle from Land's End to John O'Groats next June. Who'd like to join me?'

If I couldn't run the Marathon, then I'd have to do something equally impressive and physically demanding in order to meet my goal before turning sixty.

My daughter, her partner and I had ten months to get ready. In the end we completed the course in two weeks, pedalling a daily average of seventy-five miles and eating our way through five meals a day to keep our energy high. It was brilliant!

If you wish to achieve something in your life, aim for the stars. Imagine the goal you wish to achieve, and then multiply it into the biggest thing it could be for you.

Too many people set too low a goal for themselves. As I sat in the garden that sunny afternoon five years ago I could have said, 'Who fancies coming on a few bike rides with me?' We'd maybe have pootled around the park a few times and kidded ourselves that we'd got into cycling now.

But this is what happens over and over again. We kid ourselves. Our lazy minds tell us we can't do things that will take us out of our accustomed comfort zones. Add to that the thoughts and opinions of others around us who might be worried for our welfare, or might simply be afraid that we'll abandon them. So we give up on the dreams we might have and settle for the perceived comfort and safety of the here and now.

This type of thinking will never get us very far. Aim for the stars. Even if you don't quite reach the stars, you'll probably get as far as the moon. Go for it. So when you ask yourself the question 'What do I want to achieve?' pay very careful attention.

Beginning with the end in mind is a vital means of getting started on your journey. It's like having your holiday itinerary, or visualising your destination. It's a compelling reason to embark on your quest.

But that's not all. When you begin with the end in mind there is another important factor that comes into play. For me, planning my big physical challenge meant it had to happen before my sixtieth birthday. If I didn't anchor my goal in time it would become little more than a pipedream gathering dust in my garage next to my bike.

Beginning with the end in mind forces you to determine when the end is. And knowing this introduces the key element of time into your goal for financial freedom.

You need to be able to work within a timeframe in order to measure your progress, and in order to know whether or not you have succeeded. You need a planning window, and you need to determine how much time you must set aside each day or week or month to move you towards your goal.

In my work as a management consultant training sales teams to be more effective, I would stage an exercise that took my students into the future.

With a roll of back to front wallpaper plastered around the walls of the training room I asked them to mark on the chart the date by which they would land their biggest deals, make their biggest turnover or achieve their greatest profits. This was the point at which they would declare themselves successful.

Once consensus had been achieved on that date – usually 18 months to two years from the current date – I sent them all out of the room and told them to go away and think about the kinds of activities they would have to engage in, and by when, in order to achieve their goal by the date set.

While they were gone I would pin up a mocked up calendar which showed their date in the future, popped the champagne and got ready to receive them.

With everything prepared I then invited them back in, handing each one a glass of bubbly as they entered.

'Congratulations!' I would say. 'Two years ago we stood in this room and discussed what needed to happen in order to make us into a successful sales force. I am delighted to say that you've surpassed yourselves. You've smashed your goal!'

It's amazing how receptive people can be to role play, especially when there is champagne on offer.

The next step in the exercise was to get them to talk about what they did to achieve the goal. Notice the use of the past tense. It is much easier to describe what you have done as opposed to what you will do. In effect this then became a planning exercise. At the end of the session they had an attractive piece of reversed Anaglypta documenting some major milestones they had to achieve within their specified time period.

By beginning with the end in mind they were able to track back to the present moment and determine what action steps they needed to take immediately to put them on the right course to meet their goal.

Begin with the end in mind, then work back to the beginning.

Once you know what your planning window is, and you know which star you're aiming for, you then need to come back to the present moment and review your existing resources. These include money, time, knowledge, experience and contacts. This is when the rubber will start to hit the road, when you realise that what you're talking about achieving isn't just a pleasant daydream for a sunny afternoon around the barbecue, but a real opportunity.

Reflective questions

- By when do you wish to achieve your financial goal?
- How will you know when you've achieved your goal? Be as specific as possible regarding the income you require, and the time you wish to spend working.
- What will life be like for you once you have achieved your goal?
- Imagine yourself two years from now. You have smashed your goal and achieved the success you dreamed of. Pour yourself your favourite beverage right now by way of celebration! With this drink in hand, brainstorm all the things you *did* to achieve your goal. You could write them down on sticky notes. Once you have recorded what you *did*, put them into a timeline sequence. Suspend your judgement – everything is possible!
- This is your strategy plan. Now flesh out how you will use the resources you have available to achieve it. If you lack the resources at any time to achieve an aspect of the strategy plan, what will you do to obtain/acquire the required resource?

NOTES

[Page left blank for your reflections]

NOTES

[Page left blank for your reflections]

9

Metrics: By when could you be financially free?

Financial planner

Once you decide to embark on a journey to financial freedom, the most important thing to establish is where you are starting from.

Contrary to the Irish joke which advises not to start from here wherever you want to go, *here* is the only place you can start. So you might as well confront your reality and be totally honest about your current circumstances.

The Financial Planner template is designed to help you do just that. After the dreaming and goal setting of the last chapter, this is where you start getting into the nitty gritty.

Completing the template will give you visibility of your assets, liabilities, savings and pensions, as well as your income, essential outgoings and your net cash flow. This is your opportunity to capture your financial position in one place and create your personal balance sheet.

In order to work through it you will have to dig out your bank statements, mortgage deeds, pay slips, pension information, credit card and loan balances. This may hurt! You have to face the true reality. This is the moment for taking stock, for looking at what you really earn, spend, save and owe. The only thing to remember here is that the truth will set you free! At worst you'll be highly motivated. At best you might be pleasantly surprised.

To view the full Financial Freedom Planner please visit www.mygoalis.uk.com/mgi-resources

Here's how to complete the Financial Planner:

1. In the Assets and Income section, the first question to address is whether you own any property, including your primary residence and any buy-to-let property. Your current home is unlikely to be giving

you an income, but you may have property that you rent out, either on short or longer lets. This property will therefore be providing you with an income that is different from your employment salary.

Both types of property you own, whether residential or buy to let, may have an associated mortgage, the details of which need to be provided under the Liabilities section. You will need to know the loan balance, remaining term and the monthly repayment for each mortgage for which you are liable.

Also under Assets and Income, consider whether you have any investment bonds that provide you with any kind of financial return. Record the details on the form, being sure to highlight the capital involved in the Value column.

Other sources of income separate from your salary might include royalties, or residual payments from any leveraged opportunities you benefit from, such as multi-level marketing. Capture as much information as you can as accurately as possible in this section to get a perspective on your current rate of passive income.

2. Under liabilities, be sure to include any credit card and loan balances along with their payment terms and monthly repayment amount.

3. Review your POTS to identify what savings you have available. This may be in the form of ring-fenced money in your business, or it may be an ISA, a regular bank account, piggy bank or stash under the mattress! Whatever form your savings take at the moment, this is what you can use to create something.

Achieving financial freedom is as much about creating opportunities as it is about taking them. So even if your saving POTS look a bit bare at the moment you have the chance to review your outgoings and identify how to make savings in your current expenditure. The whole point of this financial planning exercise is to identify what opportunities you can make, however small initially.

And don't overlook the opportunity to sell on any items you own. Ebay or car-boot sales could help you generate a savings seed fund – it could be time to release cash from your attic!

4. Pensions are another form of savings and these days we are all advised to set aside money to top up our pension. Gone are the days of a reliable occupational scheme that our employer grew on our behalf.

You will particularly wish to take action on your pension fund if you are currently paying into a money purchase scheme that may not be achieving the level of growth you require to be able to sustain you in retirement. It could be time to dig out your pension policy and statements, and contact your provider to give you a transfer value. (Steel yourself first – this could be your 'Oh Shit' moment as it was mine!)

A 'frozen' pension is one that you have from a previous employer that hasn't been transferred to another scheme. If you have a 'frozen' pension, this could be a good source of investment income. Even if you are already in draw-down, as long as you have a pension pot there are still things that you can do to boost your fund and improve the level of return you can achieve.

You may also wish to consider what will happen to your pension after you die, and what provision your current pension arrangements make for your dependants. Typically, money purchase schemes die with you, leaving nothing to your survivors, or at best leaving your spouse a percentage of your pension income after you have passed away. Nevertheless, there are schemes available that are fully inheritable; if so, you may wish to think about transferring it to a fund that will better support your dependants in the future.

Unfortunately if you have purchased an annuity there is no longer a pension pot available to you as you have exchanged it for income. In this circumstance you may need to look at releasing equity from your property in order to provide investment funds.

5. Your current salary may be the only form of regular income you have. Your job is your active income generator – because you have to exchange your own time in return for your money.

Since financial freedom is about making money without exchanging your time, your aim is to grow your passive income to achieve first of all security, then independence, before finally breaking free of the rat race altogether. You will be out of the rat race when your passive income exceeds your essential and nonessential outgoings as well as your monthly liabilities, and when you find yourself planning activities on the basis of when you can fit them in as opposed to if you can afford them.

Your essential outgoings include all the things you have to pay in order to survive and keep your home. Be honest and realistic about these. At the start of your journey, and at regular intervals as you go along, it is always worth combing through your outgoings to make savings. In the early days it may be prudent to stop any nonessential luxuries, in the knowledge that you will gradually be able to reintroduce these in the future if you like.

6. Your Net Cash Flow is the figure you get when you subtract your outgoings from your income. The

relationship between your time for money income and your passive income indicates how far away you are from financial freedom.

If your cash flow is negative you are spending more than you have got coming in. For example, if your salary is £1500 and your monthly outgoings are £1750, you are spending more than you've got coming in, so your cash flow is minus £250. If you have £2500 worth of savings, you are ten months from going broke. By dividing your shortfall into your savings you can see how long you have before the money runs out. If you have no savings, you *are* broke. Remedial action is urgently required.

Client Case Study: Juliet and Andy

Juliet and Andy have been clients of mine since 2015. I think it's fair to say that for them their initial Financial Planner exercise truly opened their eyes to what was possible for them. Until they looked carefully at their financial reality they had no way of confronting the fact that they were only six weeks away from broke, with no means of working out how to improve their situation.

When I first met Juliet in summer 2014 she was a self-employed freelance writer producing articles for a local magazine, and beginning to develop her commercial writing offering. We met at a networking event and chatted about all sorts, including golf and cycling.

As a writer and journalist Juliet was adept at asking me questions about the work I did, so in response I began to explain to her a little bit about helping people make their money make money. At this point I saw the familiar look of panic sweep across Juliet's face. I mentioned how it was possible to start with a relatively small amount and gradually build it up, through investments and compounding; and how people are often pleasantly surprised by how much they do actually have in assets without fully realising it.

Looking back, it probably wasn't the best introduction! I told her the story of the father who offered his two sons the choice of £1 million right now, or a penny which would double in value every day for 30 days. Typically, when I tell this story people either glaze over, or I notice a spark in their eye and sense a curiosity to know more.

In Juliet's case, despite the panic, I sensed her curiosity about the doubling penny.

Nevertheless, after our first conversation we didn't speak for quite a few months. After meeting Juliet, I had added her to my mailing list and connected with her on social media, so she regularly received information about what My Goal Is was up to.

At the beginning of January 2015 I received an email from her. She had read my Financial Freedom pamphlet and had devoured the four books I recommend as further reading for anyone beginning their financial education journey. She wanted to meet and find out more.

In the intervening period since our first meeting, Juliet's magazine client had undergone a restructure and decided to take on staff writers instead of freelancers. Although she was averaging only £600 a month income from that client, and was far from the main breadwinner in her household, it was nevertheless a useful contribution to the family's coffers.

Having lost her regular work Juliet then decided to put extra effort into marketing her services as a commercial copywriter. She is a highly competent wordsmith, with a particular talent for assimilating complex information and communicating it in a readable and engaging way. She was looking to assist businesses with their website copy, blogs and customer success stories. It all sounded very positive, but it was still a job. Despite her competence, Juliet was limited in how much she could earn by virtue of the fact that she would only get paid when she'd done the work.

During our conversation she told me about her husband Andy, who is a very talented software engineer, also running his own business from home. While at the time he was attracting higher paying clients than Juliet, he was still trading his time for money, just like his wife. Not only that, he was regularly experiencing high levels of stress, feeling the pressure of being the main source of income in the family, and this was putting a lot of strain on their relationship.

What struck me about Juliet and Andy's story initially is that they had met at Cambridge University. I only mention this because despite achieving what could be regarded as the pinnacle of academic training, and having both grown up in professional families, by their own admission they had really no idea about how to improve their personal wealth. In a nutshell, they may have received the best academic education available, yet their financial understanding was zilch.

Now in their mid to late forties, they had both previously pursued corporate careers and had been running their own professional services businesses for the past ten to fifteen years: businesses that would cease to operate if anything happened to either of them.

So they were far from financially free.

Juliet in particular was feeling this pain. She told me: 'I've never wanted to be dependent on anyone. I want to be free to spend time writing without worrying where my next pay cheque is coming from but at the moment this feels like an impossible dream.'

By the time Juliet came to play the Cash Flow Game with us, she was fully engaged with her own financial education. The penny, doubled or not, was starting to drop. She said:

'I was beginning to find out from Neil about different alternative investment schemes with predictable, fixed returns, but at this point I wasn't really sure how Andy would respond. So many people have the attitude that if it looks too good to be true it probably is, and at the time I was fully expecting Andy to be of a similar mind.

'I can't remember exactly how I brought the subject up, but eventually I persuaded Andy to read one or two of the books that Neil had recommended. He started to get interested in what we might do to improve our situation, and for the first time in years we sat down together and went through all of our outgoings. I guess we were both guilty of sticking our head in the sand and hoping for the best. But if we were going to embark on a journey to financial freedom it was important to know exactly how much money we needed just to be able to pay our monthly expenses.'

In their eagerness to improve their financial education Juliet and Andy had bought a well-known personal wealth coaching programme. They attended a number of the coaching calls and read through a lot of the material. Juliet said:

'In hindsight it was probably an unnecessary expense which ironically did cause us quite a cash flow headache for a few months! But at the time it did get us thinking and talking about what we would like to achieve. It also got us looking carefully at our existing assets, liabilities and expenses, so that when we went to talk to Neil in more detail we were a bit more clued up about what we had available.'

Juliet and Andy worked out that they needed at least £3000 every month to cover their expenses. But they owned their house outright and both had an amount of frozen pension money saved up from their corporate employment days.

Neither of them was looking to retire soon – they both love their work, and as self-employed professionals there is nothing preventing them from continuing to work for however long they wish.

However, Juliet's final salary scheme pension was only likely to pay her between £8000 and £13000 per annum on her retirement, while Andy's pension pot was even less favourable. They would almost certainly have to sell the family home in order to fund their retirement unless they did something different with their cash.

'I was excited about the opportunities Neil was describing to us,' Andy said. 'I appreciated Neil's down-to-earth approach and how he encouraged us to research the investments for ourselves. I got more and more curious about the possibilities and was amazed at how I'd never really appreciated some pretty simple things about money that I was now learning.'

In terms of timescale, Juliet and Andy have about fifteen years before they might be ready to consider retiring, and with a medium attitude to risk this gives them plenty of time to grow pension pots in excess of £1 million. They elected to transfer their funds into a Group Small Self-Administered Scheme which yields well over ten times their original providers, as well as providing inheritance benefits.

In addition to this, Andy came up with a more aggressive plan to generate enough passive income to cover their monthly expenses within the next couple of years. He explained:

'I'd love to be captain of our golf club before I get invited to play in the seniors when I'm 55! I've loved the game since I was a boy and would relish the opportunity as captain to play as much as I could, as well as host others in the game and raise money for charity in the process. But when I have to work so much just to put food on the table this is obviously a very difficult thing to achieve. At the moment I feel very limited by my job.

'Having satisfied myself about the schemes that Neil had mentioned, I initially thought about remortgaging the house to reinvest. I had learned about borrowing to invest on our coaching programme so felt that it was entirely possible, if higher risk.

'I have to admit to feeling extremely relieved that none of the lenders were interested in considering our application, not even for twenty per cent of the value of our home and not even in principle,' Juliet said. 'I guess this is where The System saved my sanity for a change!'

Just like anyone embarking on this journey, Juliet and Andy needed to understand the dynamic between their available resources, timescale and attitude to risk. With a lot of resources and a lot of time, our attitude to risk doesn't have to be high. But with fewer resources and a shorter time period available to us our attitude to risk needs to be on the high side in order to achieve good returns more quickly.

With Juliet's more cautious approach the couple's risk attitude had to be described as medium. She explained:

'Whilst I am in favour of investing in properly researched alternatives, there is a part of me which is slightly more risk averse than my husband. He thinks things through super quick, whereas I take a longer time to process and understand things. I need examples and reassurances. I also need to feel that our capital is protected.'

During their financial review Juliet and Andy remembered that they had a mortgage endowment maturing in three years' time. When they first took out this insurance it was against a £50,000 mortgage on their first home, but they knew that it wasn't going to be worth that amount on maturity. They decided to find out how much it would be if they released it earlier than its full term and were told it was now worth £30,000.

'It's interesting that if we had needed that money to pay off our mortgage we would have been extremely disappointed that it had depreciated by forty per cent of its original value. But as a dotcom windfall in the early noughties had enabled us to pay off our mortgage the endowment now represented free capital.

'We decided to invest it in a scheme that is making five per cent a month, so by the rule of 72 it will have doubled its value in just over fourteen months, and will then be covering our expenses. So I guess Andy could be sharpening up his golf game ready for captaincy in a couple of years – well before his fifty-fifth birthday!'

Juliet and Andy's story is typical of families who are working hard to earn, but who consequently never have very much time to devote to the things they enjoy doing – like creative writing or golf.

Often making money make money is more about releasing your time rather than expanding your material wealth.

Who	Resources	Time	Attitude to risk	Outcome
Juliet and Andy	Cash + Pension + House (mortgage free)	*15 years to retirement *2 years to covering expenses passively	Medium	*Invested cash to achieve partial income within 60 days *Pension growing 20% pa *House remains mortgage free

Once you have clear visibility of your financial position, you may well begin to feel motivated to improve it. Allow yourself half an hour a day to work on your finances.

NOTES

[Page left blank for your reflections]

10

Make money make money: What are you going to do to achieve financial freedom?

You have your vision of where you hope to get to and you know where you're starting from. You know that you want to generate more passive income, and you may well have a clear picture that you want to do more charitable or creative projects that aren't job dependent.

Perhaps you have your sights set on becoming a property investor. You imagine that you are going to make money from buy-to-let or multi-occupancy development. You quite like the idea of owning holiday rental property abroad, giving you a reason to travel to places that you love. Or you might prefer to renovate property in disrepair and flip it to make a capital return.

Maybe you have the mindset of an entrepreneur, and you are interested in developing your own business, either from scratch, or by leveraging an existing organisational infrastructure and network, such as in multi-level marketing. You enjoy helping people develop, and you love meeting and interacting with new people all the time. You've noticed the great lifestyle that multi-level marketing representatives enjoy, and you envisage yourself in a similar role, benefiting from corporate-like, incentivised training and development, as well as a residual income from growing your network.

Alternatively, you may have quite a numerical mind and you enjoy keeping track of the financial news. You've always been attracted to the thrill of stock market gains, and you are skilled at analysing markets and companies to spot the upcoming investment opportunities. You would enjoy working from home and trading in your own paper-based assets. You decide that you are going to make your money work for you by learning how to trade and how to take proper advantage of stock market.

All of these income generators require activity on your part: managing tenants, restoring property, following the markets and networking. They are good opportunities to develop new skills and introduce you to a new group of like-minded individuals, as well as make you money.

But what if you simply don't have the time or the energy to invest in these types of activity?

What if, when you've come home from a hard day at your job, you have a quick bite to eat then scoot off out to plaster walls, meet investors or train your recruits, instead of playing with your children or spending time with friends and family?

Does this mean you have no chance of increasing your income?

No!

One option is to look for *passive* income generator opportunities.

Passive generators require no input from you once the investment is made. They usually have a defined return at a specific point in time. Some make one-off returns, while others make returns monthly or quarterly.

Examples of passive generators include joint venture property investment, packaged trading opportunities and packaged alternative investments.

The most crucial element in all such opportunities is to conduct thorough due diligence on the prospective partners, managers and funds. But, once you are comfortable with the individuals involved, and have a clear understanding of how the investments work, including their associated risks, you need take no further action after the investment is made.

These types of opportunity suit serious investors with no knowledge or experience in property, trading and investment portfolios and with little time to actively manage their investments themselves.

By improving your own financial awareness, and by conducting the appropriate level of due diligence, you can ensure that these are not too-good-to-be-true scams, as popular opinion might have them.

Once you begin to make the returns you will start to find out exactly how it feels to wake up every day and be free to choose what you want to do with your day.

Another cautionary tale

How passive you want your income to be is an important question to tackle. It requires knowing your own strengths and weaknesses, and appreciating what else your job or other income generating activity gives you as well as money.

My client who wishes to remain anonymous learned a little too late about what full time employment actually meant to him, and he needed to reassess what he had to do to replace certain elements of his job after he had sacked the boss.

Ironically, the very thing that he'd yearned for at the beginning of his journey – more time – was the thing that knocked him back.

'I wanted to be free of the time for money trap. The company I was working for wanted their pound of flesh and I desperately wanted

to be rid of it. However, although I didn't really want to be spending so much of my time driving and selling, as a serial procrastinator the last thing I needed really was more time!

'I'm missing the routine of work if I'm honest. I didn't realise how much I'd come to rely on the structure that the nine to five gave me, nor indeed the level of social interaction. Not having much of a social circle outside work meant that when I left I actually felt quite isolated.'

Originally my client's plan after leaving the corporate world was to set himself up as a mentor for others who wished to leave the rat race too. However, after launching his new website he received a few comments from people objecting to having their nose rubbed in his financial success. It was a big lesson, and with his change of personal circumstances he didn't feel that he was entirely in the right place to be offering help to others.

'I have since learned that the more time I have the less I do! I didn't have a clear enough plan of what I was going to spend my time on after full time employment came to an end. The mentor idea had seemed a good one, but I didn't feel I was entirely in the right place myself to be offering help to others.'

As well as the lack of structure and social interaction without the need to work, my client also became aware of a sense of vulnerability.

'Not only is it difficult to explain to people how you get by without a job, you also begin to feel slightly outside society. People make their own judgements about money, and there was a period where I would spend a lot of time elaborating on what I was doing to earn income, which a lot of people made a snap judgement on.

'There were also times where people would approach me to invest in their property scheme, on the strength of their perception that I had a load of spare cash. It's possible to feel like a bit of a target sometimes.'

Despite his harsh lessons, however, my client feels that what he has achieved over the past twelve months has been all to the good.

'It wasn't really until I met Neil that I even started to question what I was doing with my time, and what I wanted for my future. All I knew was that I had to try and make money in other ways than through my job, which was taking such a massive toll on my health.

'It has certainly been a rocky road, and I know there are still some challenges ahead as I stabilise my income and my capital. However, I have at least taken the time to do lots of reading and enhance my personal development. I have also taken stock of my mistakes, so eventually I'll be able to advise others about how to avoid them in their own journey.

'One of the first things to do is to get comfortable with not having to work! And then come up with an explanation that people will accept about why you don't have to work. The key here is not to say too much! These days I just explain that I have some property investments and that's it. People are usually either too shy or too puzzled to ask any more questions after that!'

I think it's fair to say that my client's bid to escape the rat race happened a little too quickly and perhaps with not enough of a plan to cover all eventualities. It may be the case that he has to re-enter employment to tide him over and allow himself a bit more time to decide what he really wants to do – and how to make it happen.

And it could be that his experience right now is the best thing that could happen to him and his future mentoring clients, as he is learning so much the hard way.

Reflective questions

- What are you going to do to make your money make money?
- How active or passive do you wish your investments to be?
- What choices are you making around your current employment?
- How will you structure your time?
- How will ensure you remain socially connected?

NOTES

[Page left blank for your reflections]

NOTES

[Page left blank for your reflections]

11

Means: How are you going to achieve financial freedom?

So, you are now clear that you are going to escape from the rat race and make money make money; you are going to achieve the mindset and circumstances of a wealthy individual; and you are going to realise your dream of being able to choose exactly how you spend your time without exchanging it for cash.

You have a clear objective in mind and you know the timescale that you are working to. Really, you could not be clearer about exactly what you are going to achieve.

The problem, however, lies not in the vision you have – but in the actions you are taking in order to get to where you want to be.

Having a vision is important – but unless you have a plan of action to achieve it it's dead in the water.

You need to set the flywheel of your financial freedom project in motion. In short, you need to do something – anything – to get it moving.

Thirty minutes a day

What does it take to change your life? Could you do it in thirty minutes a day?

Remember the power of compounding. Starting with a regular financial-freedom focused activity each day for thirty minutes will get you into the right frame of mind to start transforming your circumstances.

Whatever we want to achieve in life we seem to be conditioned into thinking that we have to earn it. And earning stuff suggests slog. It's difficult to escape the notion that transforming your life is likely to take a huge effort, a lot of commitment and cast iron discipline.

Say you want to run a marathon in a couple of years' time, but right now you struggle to run for a bus. You wouldn't carry on sitting around until a week before the race then suddenly jump up and start training would you? Neither would you set off today to attempt the entire twenty-six miles.

Nevertheless, with the right plan and the right pace there is every chance that you will be successful in achieving your goal.

In a financial context, your 'marathon' could be to achieve an income of £100,000 in two years' time – without doing any more work. You know that you've missed the boat on your savings; and unless you win the lottery or come into an inheritance you can't expect the capital to materialise out of nowhere.

So there has to be a different way for you to meet your target.

In the same way as training for a big race, now is the time to put in place the right plan at the right pace.

Pace is an important word. It refers to action over time: action that is sustainable, so you can keep it going for as long as possible. This applies as much to growing your wealth as it does your fitness. You want it to feel easy. You don't want it to feel like a slog. It has to be a straightforward thing to introduce into your life's busy schedule – and you have to feel motivated.

For many of us motivation comes from the future, from the person we wish to become, or from a dearly held dream we wish to achieve.

For some it comes in a lightning flash – a change of attitude, a sudden burst of gratitude and a desire to live life to the full.

For others of us, who are perhaps comfortable enough in our current existence, the motivation is more problematic. 'After a hard day at work, I can't be bothered. Anyway, I'd miss *Eastenders*.'

But let's say you're prepared to take a big enough leap towards achieving your dream that you are prepared to forgo your favourite soap. Let's say you are going to change your life – and all you've got is thirty minutes a day, or three and a half hours a week.

Is it possible?

A saying that has been doing the rounds of cyberspace over the past few years is 'what you focus on grows'. It's a bit of a cliché, but like all good clichés it does hold its own wisdom.

Focusing on improving your financial education, even for thirty minutes a day, means that over time your understanding will increase. And once this happens you will want to find opportunities to put your knowledge into practice.

You'll quickly discover that there are more options available to you than simply the nine to five with the consolation of *Eastenders* in the evening.

Even consolidating all your thirty minutes for one week into three and a half hours, and using the time to attend an investors' networking meeting, would catapult you a long way towards your goal by virtue of what you can learn from others and the contacts you would make.

Some of my My Goal Is clients generate healthy amounts of passive income through their involvement in multi-level marketing businesses (read more about this later in Section Two). They spend their thirty minutes a day making calls, enrolling their contacts, and building further income generating teams.

Others work on their own business, and create opportunities to generate passive income from their own products and services.

Still others might spend half an hour scanning the stock market for investment opportunities, and conducting due diligence on schemes that others in their network have recommended.

Really, once you commit to spending thirty minutes each day focusing on what you wish to grow, the sky is the limit. Just like training for a marathon, getting fit and race ready is a matter of time, but more importantly, it's also a matter of sustained and repeated action and commitment – even just a small amount each and every day.

If you're now wondering where on earth you can start, and what on earth you would spend your daily half hour on, rest assured that reading this book is an important first step. You have already made a start. Even by spending a few minutes a day reading about financial freedom means that you are moving towards making your vision a reality. There is a further reading section in the back of this book detailing other titles you will find useful.

Choosing not to listen to your current friends and other influences in your life who will tell you to stay safe, and not fall for things that sound too good to be true, is another important, if tricky step.

Meeting new people who are on a similar path is another approach.

For some people kicking off their journey to financial freedom really will require an 'oh shit' moment. This will be an occasion where realisation dawns that they are not going to have quite as much money in retirement as they imagined, or that their ambitions to do something with their life are nothing but pipe dreams.

As long as you have started moving, your progress could leapfrog. Your trajectory to financial freedom may not move in a straight line. But it will move in some direction as long as you start.

Once you've read as much as you can stomach, applied the ear plugs and spoken to a few people about their own approaches to growing their wealth, it's time to graduate from research into action.

Here are some key next steps with which to fill your daily thirty minutes.

Sort out your personal finances.

You've got to know where you are and where you are starting from. You need to set out what income you've got, and what you're spending it on.

So make yourself a chart, like the following:

Name:			
Monthly income:			
Expenditure items	Current Spend	% Income	What could you get by on?
Gas/Oil			
Electricity			
Water			
Telephone Fixed			
Telephone Mobile			
Television			
Broadband			
Food consumed at home			
Eating out			
Take-aways			
Other			

entertainment			
Gym/self-care			
Clothes			
Holidays			
Fuel			
Car insurance			
Car tax			
Car maintenance			
Home insurance			
Life insurance			
Medical insurance			
Credit card repayments			
Pets			
Home maintenance			
Garden			
Subscriptions			
Memberships			
Hobbies			
School fees			

The key to this exercise is to be honest. This way you will be able to work out what proportion of your income you spend each month, and get some insights into what you could actually get by on.

For example, if you are in the habit of spending £2.99 on a latte every working day, then already you can identify a weekly saving of £14.95, or £777.40 over the whole year, by choosing to drink a glass of tap water instead. What might you do with that saving? You might even improve your health!

The difference between the amount you spend and the amount you could get by on gives you the amount you could save or invest each month.

Next, look at where you have money locked up that you could release. Do you have clothes you've never worn? Items you could sell?

What choices are you making? Are you choosing Sky over Freeview? Preparing meals from scratch or buying ready meals? How many cars do you have? Do you really need one? If so does it really have to be a top of the range vehicle? How are you financing it?

The key is to take a deep breath, stop for a while and look carefully at what you are doing. Are you secretly relying on a windfall to create the funds you want?

If you want to stay in the rat race then buy the designer stuff and drive a bigger car – but recognise that you will be forever spending what you earn and staying just over broke. This is what The System wants! And if you're spending more than you earn you are either depleting your capital or increasing your debt, as outlined by the POTS Model in Section One.

People often don't realise what they're spending and are often driven to keep up with the Joneses. But just because you pay more for things doesn't always mean it's the best. For example, on a recent reality TV show which forced participants to confront their addiction to brand buying, it was actually Asda's own brand toilet paper that came out tops over the famous, and more expensive, Andrex!

It's time to take stock and ask yourself whether you are falling for the illusions advertisers are creating. Is what you want the same as what you need?

If you are confusing want with need without the means to pay for it then you are likely to be a long way from living the dream – and it could turn into a nightmare unless you are in control.

If you are prudent and have pared down your expenses but still can't find the funds you need to save or invest, can you borrow? Can you leverage other people's money, time or network to run a business on the side of your current job? The section on leveraging will be especially useful in explaining the principles of using other people's resources to generate profit for yourself.

Always pay yourself first

Treat your budget with respect and make sure you allocate enough funds to cover the essentials. In the same way that a self-employed individual must cover their costs and overheads you must put aside the proper amount to satisfy your living expenses.

Perhaps the axiom 'always pay yourself first' is more immediately meaningful to people who are self-employed and who have a very real sense of what it means to pay themselves. Employees tend to wait for their pay cheque then spend as usual. They don't necessarily apply the concept of covering their budget first. They don't necessarily have a budget.

A more business-like approach to personal money management really helps in taking control. Spending blind makes you poor. Having visibility of your outgoings will help you to budget and grow your wealth. In fact, you might be very surprised how the simple act of taking stock of your current circumstances immediately improves your situation. If what you focus on grows, focusing on your finances will bring you more wealth.

Once you have covered the basics there is nothing wrong with setting aside 'enjoyment money' too – as long as you don't push yourself into needless debt.

Emulating the POTS Model will help you take control. You should have different bank accounts – one for living, one for luxuries and one for savings and investments.

The key here is to physically move your money into the relevant account and ring-fence it. If you don't, then you are at risk of eating into your capital.

Consistently grow your wealth

By regularly putting money away to earn interest you will benefit from the mathematical wonder of compounding. Sadly, the amount of interest generally available on the High Street is pitiful, and the amount of years it will take you to double your money in that environment could possibly far exceed your natural life span. Revisit the Rule of 72 and the principle of compounding in Section One.

However, just understanding that patience and discipline work hand in hand with the compounding effect is an important first step. When you double a penny a day, after ten days you end up with £5.12, but after thirty days you end up with over £10 million! Understanding that the big results come at the end of the savings period ought to encourage you to let your money grow, and to be consistent in what you do.

Build your support team

You need to think about the individuals who will work with you to advise, support and challenge you on your journey. As we have shown this is best not to be a regulated professional, or a friend or family member in your existing circle. So you will need to widen your net in order to identify experienced, like-minded individuals.

You could try reaching out to established training programmes, such as Robert and Kim Kiyosaki's Rich Dad Coaching scheme. Or, more locally and cost effectively, you could look for Cash Flow Game groups in your area, or set one up yourself.

If you are particularly keen on developing a portfolio of property assets, the Property Mastery Academy could be for you. There are also numerous property investor networking groups around the country where you can listen to experienced individuals and meet like-minded people.

If you're interested in building a part-time business, you might consider the option of network or multi-level marketing.

If you would like to find out how to take greater control over your financial circumstances but simply don't know where to start, you could do worse than talk to us here at My Goal Is to find out what could be possible for you.

Outsource to others

In business, companies often buy in necessary services to save them having to employ staff to undertake them. It often works out to be more cost effective to pay a freelancer or an outsourcing partner to do anything from accounts to systems and facilities management.

On a personal level you might get someone in to decorate your home or maintain your garden. This is also outsourcing a project that you could probably do yourself if you had the time or the inclination. Often the cost of the service is vastly outweighed by the speed, quality and convenience delivered by the professionals. True there are some cowboys out there, but as long as you feel you have been treated respectfully and fairly and are happy with the result then you will always feel that you have received value for money.

Similarly, when it comes to managing our finances we have to be wary of the cowboys. However, even reputable advisors and financial institutions can leave you less than satisfied with the way your money is managed. It isn't necessarily that you have recruited a third party to advise you or invest your money that is the risky bit. The biggest risk factor lies in your own level of financial understanding. Even a small amount of financial awareness will enable you to ask some questions. If you have no understanding at all – and especially if you also have a lot of fear around asking 'dumb' questions – then you are putting yourself in an extremely vulnerable position.

Over the past twenty years there has been much controversy about how financial products have been foisted upon individuals whose level of understanding made them targets for unscrupulous commission driven sales tactics. I meet many people who have at one time or another had their ignorance and cautious approach exploited to tie them into high premium, low performing products.

But there is always a way to insulate ourselves from such risks – and it is to raise our own awareness, understanding and curiosity.

The ability to ask questions is crucial. But so is knowing which questions to ask – and this will only come with learning something about how products are structured, how they come to market and what alternatives exist.

If you wish to transform your financial circumstances and achieve freedom from your current hamster wheel, you're going to have to resist the temptation to hand over your money blindly to somebody else, for example an , and ask them to look after it for you, without doing any homework of your own.

Even if you do decide to outsource your wealth management it is important to understand exactly what your chosen service provider can do for you. Independent Financial Advisors can only talk to you about regulated products, but any investments you make with them will be covered by the Financial Services Compensation Scheme. You will have to accept the returns you are offered, and that your capital can go down as well as up.

The thing to remember is that just because a product is regulated does not make it a lower risk investment. In fact, some of the most secure investments, such as property where there is a first charge on an underpinning asset, are unregulated. In this type of Alternative Investment no-one can give you advice because the products and opportunities are not regulated. In that sense you are on your own. By contrast the majority of the regulated market is trading speculatively in stocks and shares. There are no underpinning assets and there can be a high degree of market volatility which puts your capital at risk.

When you put yourself in the position whereby you are able to make your own informed decisions about how to manage your money, you are really beginning to take control of your wealth — and you stand a better chance of reaping the benefits yourself rather than having to pay management fees to a third party.

Other outsourcing options include joint ventures. These are usually deals associated with property. For example, you could lend money to a property investor and achieve a first charge on the asset. You could then make one–two per cent interest a month on your loan.

Alternatively, you might do a deal which gives you a monthly share of the property's rental income, or you might get involved in a flip, where you loan money to purchase a property, then obtain a share of the profit once a property is sold, plus the return of your capital.

If you work with the right people you can make significant returns through both income and capital growth.

If your goal is to make passive income, joint ventures with property investors are definitely worth considering as you don't have to do anything other than provide the capital and wait for the pay-out.

But once again it is vital to know exactly who it is you are dealing with and what their level of experience is. If you don't have any experience yourself or a clear understanding of how property deals work then you are still going to be vulnerable in this market without conducting your own due diligence.

So it is important to remember the difference between outsourcing part of your income generation because you have taken an informed decision to benefit from leveraging versus outsourcing because you can't really be bothered to find out much yourself.

Outsourcing should definitely play a role in your investment portfolio. It can give you the ability to invest in areas where you don't have the knowledge or the expertise, simultaneously striking a delicate balance between careless ignorance and informed passivity.

If you only ever invest in areas where you feel comfortable – such as property – then you are playing a risky game. Putting all your eggs in the same basket is always a flawed strategy over the longer term, so outsourcing is a good way of making more asset classes available to you for you to de-risk your portfolio.

Shifting attitude to risk

As you grow your wealth your attitude to risk will change. Most people are surprised to see themselves become more risk averse. You may then decide to protect some of your wealth by investing in regulated product.

Who will invest your money on your behalf? And how safe is it?

The first thing most people think about is opening a savings account in a bank. At the time of writing the best rate of interest that can be achieved through this is not much better than two per cent fixed over two years. The fact that there are some current accounts offering five per cent per year for a minimum deposit of £1000 per month, and the fact that there have been some tax concessions on interest payable in 2016, are testament to the need to keep cash liquidity in The System.

Regarding safety, the first £75,000 in each account holder's name is safe, guaranteed by the Financial Services Compensation Scheme, as we mentioned earlier.

Individual Savings Accounts or ISAs are tax-free savings platforms offered to retail investors. Again your money is protected by the and is subject to the same £75,000 guarantee as above. The interest rates offered are little more than two per cent per annum, but ISAs do offer a way of making savings tax efficient.

Independent Financial Advisors will invest your funds in 'whole of market' regulated products and opportunities for a fee. They too are covered by the Financial Services Compensation Scheme, but often have signed a clause acknowledging that your capital is at risk of decreasing as well as increasing, so you have effectively given your consent for it to diminish! Independent Financial Advisors often direct their clients to schemes based in the volatile and speculative stocks and shares market, which although regulated may not always offer fixed returns over predetermined periods.

Joint venture partners, be they friends or family or strangers, all require careful monitoring and due diligence if you are to trust them with your capital. These types of investment opportunities are unlikely to be regulated, so they will not be subject to any guarantee or compensation scheme. You will have to identify alternative ways to protect your capital – such as securing a first charge over the underpinning asset, or investigating ways to achieve a capital guarantee. None the less, it is worth opening your mind to this kind of wealth creation – and be aware that the majority of people who seem to be making good money around you are probably investing in the unregulated market such as property or packaged trading and investment opportunities.

Do it yourself

The whole point of this book is to give you sufficient knowledge, information, motivation, inspiration and courage to take control of your own financial future yourself.

And if you are committed to this course of action in order to achieve financial freedom you will quickly find that you needn't be alone for long. If you go out looking for like-minded people you will find that there are networks of individuals with whom you can connect who are already investing for themselves and are already making significant strides towards their own financial freedom.

By working through the steps in this book you will be able to identify what works for you and your risk profile.

Yes, you could leap off the ten metre diving board straight away; but you might choose to jump in off the side first of all. That's also fine. The principle is never to put in more money than you can afford to lose to start with.

It's good to get into the habit of conducting regular financial health checks. These can happen as soon as you wish to evaluate your current position, and may at first involve a review of your own expenses and liabilities as well as your strategy to save. Once you have identified spare money that you can grow you will thereafter be checking the health of your assets and investments along with your attitude to risk. It will be vital to know when the risks change, and when the investment terms, structures and conditions change.

Leveraging

One of the mechanisms of finance that it is worth getting to grips with is that of leveraging. It is effectively borrowing other people's money to invest and make profits for yourself. And before you get twitchy about it, it's what the banks do every night with your money without even asking you.

Leveraging means using something that doesn't belong to you to create an end result for yourself that is far greater than the cost incurred in using the thing. It's not just limited to money either. You might make use of another person's time, equipment or network to leverage your own returns.

This might sound like exploitation – but that's what interest payments are for. They enable the lender to increase their loan capital over the term of the loan at a reasonable rate – effectively making money out of the money loaned to you.

For example, I borrow £100 off a friend for twelve months and agree to pay him five per cent interest over the year on his loan. I then use the money to buy raw materials to make cakes. Over the course of the year I end up with £1000 in my bank account following the sale of the cakes I have made. I repay the loan I owe to my friend with interest, leaving me with £895. Had I used my own £100 I would have made a tenfold return, but since I used another person's money and made more profit than the cost of borrowing then I have leveraged my friend's loan to make an infinite return.

A simple way of thinking about leveraging is that you are using other people's money to make money for yourself. Mortgages are the most common example.

The biggest caveat here is to be careful about borrowing to invest. In fact, my own rule of personal money management is not to do it!

However, it is worth looking at as interest rates on borrowing have never been so low. Ten year fixed rate mortgages cost under three per cent – currently Barclays will lend ten-year money at 2.99 per cent!

So surely if I can invest the cash and obtain a far higher return over a decade I'm fine?

But we are no longer in a normal world. When we see banks prepared to lend money at 2.99 per cent for ten years the proof of this is staring us in the face.

So, could you borrow money at those low rates and then do something with the money you've borrowed to make a profit?

In the early noughties we saw something like this happening – but not because interest rates were low. At that time there were crazy credit card lenders prepared to advance massive credit balances for nothing. These took the form of zero per cent transfer deals. It was easy to grab the cash and put it in your savings account.

Others took the cash and used it to purchase property to rent out. At the time house prices were rising and they were able to refinance the property in order to pay back the credit card when the zero per cent deal ended.

But here's the cautionary tale – some people got caught out when property prices crashed in 2008!

You can't do this on credit cards now, the transfer fees just kill the returns. But can you do it with a mortgage?

Yes, you can – but you're unlikely to profit if you don't like risk.

The current best five year deposit account available in the High Street pays just 3.02 per cent before tax. There's no head room here if you are borrowing from Barclays at 2.99 per cent.

You are going to have to move a little further up the risk scale. You might even consider unregulated asset-backed products offering a minimum return of seven to eight per cent before tax.

These opportunities tend to have terms of between fifteen months and seven years, which means you would have to find something else for your money once the term runs out. But I'm very confident that similar products would be available.

Then there's buy-to-let. Many of our clients have buy-to-let properties in their portfolio. Returns on investment in excess of ten per cent per annum are very achievable.

Here, you would use the cash you have borrowed as deposits and gear up again with a buy-to-let mortgage. Buy-to-let mortgages typically run to a maximum of seventy-five per cent of the property price. So if you borrowed £100,000, you'd have around £400,000 to spend on one or more properties (£100,000 cash plus £300,000 from mortgages).

Wow, this is getting exciting! Having a mortgage offer available for such a long period at an amazingly low rate does get you thinking.

(Remember, if this all sounds far too exciting for you, you can stick with regulated products. Make an appointment to see your friendly IFA, pay their fees and take the regulated returns and pay more fees!)

Multi-level marketing

Another example of leveraging is making use of other people's time and network. Multi-level marketing, or network businesses use this model enabling individuals to recruit others and subsequently make small percentages of what those below them make.

It is possible to get going in multi-level marketing (MLM) for a relatively small amount of money, essentially investing in the product or service the organisation provides, and then building a team around you to promote it.

There are plenty of MLM organisations out there and one of them would be right for you.

Take a look at companies such as: -

- Utility Warehouse
- Arbonne
- Forever Living
- USANA Health Sciences
- Herbalife
- Neal's Yard Remedies
- Avon

Just because you have no money to start with doesn't mean you can't start your journey to financial freedom. You just need to take the first step!

Key points about MLM:

- It requires you to actively promote products and
- recruit and motivate a network below you
- It allows you to leverage the time of others
- It does not always require significant initial outlay
- It is not asset backed
- It primarily produces income
- It doesn't require a good credit history
- Support is often available from up lines.

Here's the case of Andy, who made the shift from employment to part time, leveraged business ownership.

Andy is a retired police officer who has always been driven to achieve better than his colleagues, peers and forebears. He became involved in multi-level marketing while still in full time employment with the police force. After retiring in June 2012 he had more time to focus on growing his MLM business and, with his pension, his investments and his passive income from his networked business, he is beginning to realise his financial freedom and dreams.

I met Andy in January 2014 when he expressed an interest in Alternatives investing. Even while working in the police force he had always done side projects to try to increase his income. So he had been involved in an online lottery syndicate, had invested in his own education about stocks and shares, and had owned a number of buy-to-let properties.

As a driven individual he had always been ready to take advantage of opportunities to help him get ahead. Here's why:

'I always had a wish to make myself solvent having seen my Dad try many things and never find the magic pill. When my Dad died he had no life insurance. Mum had to move out of the house. I vowed never to allow the people I leave behind to be in that situation, so I've always looked for ways to improve things financially for myself and my daughters.'

Having sold all his properties at the time of the recession in 2008, Andy was on the look-out for a new way to work on his fortune when a colleague of his introduced him to a British, FTSE 250 listed services-based multi-level marketing company.

The opportunity involved acquiring both customers and distributors. When you sign up customers you make a certain amount of commission on their registration, and then a percentage of their monthly spend on services. When you recruit distributors you make commission on the services their customers buy every month.

Reflecting on the opportunity Andy said: 'For me it was the ideal company. It was offering services that everyone already uses on a daily basis, which suited me as I couldn't be approaching people I know to spend money on items they don't need purely to feather my nest.

'It also offers consumers an excellent way of making savings on services they are already using, and if they want to take the further step to becoming distributors it gives them a way of making money passively too.

'These days most people I speak to about the business and its offering are happy when I leave their house because I've either saved them money or they know where their finances lie, and have an opportunity to grow their income.'

When Andy first started with MLM he was two and a half years away from retirement. He said:

'I hated having a boss and I hated that I only had twenty six days' holiday a year. It wasn't enough! Holidays are my passion! I love travelling and I wanted to achieve a situation in my life where I could take as many holidays as I wished.'

At the beginning Andy put in three to five hours a week on his new venture. This involved making appointments with people already in his circle to tell them about the savings they could make and the money they could earn, and how they could get started.

'When I started, a typical day meant working my full time job, teaching photography part time, spending time with my two daughters, and making sure I didn't miss my workout at the gym. It was already quite a busy life, but I knew that in order to get to where I wanted to go I needed to put the effort in.

'I aimed to conduct three appointments a week at the beginning. It can be the hardest thing to do after a full day's work to drag yourself out of the chair in the evening and go to an appointment. But if you don't do it you don't achieve anything. And some of those early appointments were amongst the best meetings I've ever had! They certainly provided the impetus and motivation to keep going.'

Andy's effort at the beginning is a great example of the compound effect at play. He recognised that MLM is an occupation that provides the flexibility to be either full or part time, but not 'some-time', in the words of entrepreneurial author and speaker Darren Hardy. It's not a truly passive income stream to begin with, but like most low-risk things in life, the more you put in, the more you get out.

'Once you put the effort in you realise that MLM grows exponentially. In the early days it's tempting to wonder whether it's all worth it. But if you plan a five to eight year period of putting in five to ten hours a week, you can have the choice of what you want to do in life. In five to ten years you could be financially free on three to five thousand a month or more through part time working.

'You've got to be fairly self-disciplined to make a go of it. But once you do that eventually the business takes on a mind of its own. Over time I discovered that referrals are the pot of gold at the end of the rainbow. If you can get people already in your network to tell their friends and colleagues about you then you're laughing. But you do have to put in the leg work to stay on the radar. You have to make the phone calls and go for the coffees. And you have to keep in mind what you're doing it all for.'

Andy is quite convinced that one of the things that he's gained most from in getting involved with MLM is the personal development element.

'In my old job I used to think that personal development was soft, fluffy, pink rubbish. Back then it was about being told what to do! But in order to establish your own network marketing business you quickly find that developing yourself into a self-starter is the most important thing.

'I always hated being told what to do anyway! I hated having a boss, so when I started reading personal development books and realising that some of the most famous and most successful individuals behaved in particular ways that contributed to their success I wanted to know more. I loved that I was reading positive stuff that was inspiring me rather than telling me what to do.'

Andy has nothing but praise for the support MLM offers. He said:

'One of the things the best MLM companies are great at is training and team-building events. These give you a great boost as well as putting you in touch with like-minded people who are experiencing similar challenges in setting up their business network. It's a very special feeling to be wanted by a group of fun-loving, goal-driven people.'

One word of caution, which seems to be a common theme amongst many individuals who decide to follow their own path to financial freedom, is that people will quickly dole out their opinion on what you're doing.

Commenting on this, Andy said:

'You do have to develop a bit of a rhino skin. I've been told by close friends and family members alike that I've been brainwashed and that I've joined a cult.

'In response I say that if I've been brainwashed it's helped me make a decision to be in the cult of something that is going to improve my life and the inheritance of my daughters. My business is willable. As it grows it will take on a mind of its own. Passive income will continue throughout the generations for as long as the business exists.'

MLM is a business model that is wholly replicable and which relies on leverage in order to grow and be successful. Andy learned the hard way that while it was OK for him to stamp his own personality on the business, there was absolutely no point in trying to improve what was already available.

'As a highly competitive individual I often want to see if I can make things better than they appear. So at first I was adding extra pages to the company presentation, in order to say more about the opportunity to prospects.

'It didn't work! I was trying to be clever but all I did was take something that worked and broke it.

'The thing that makes MLM work is that it can be duplicated. This is why it's easy for people to join in. It's all about using a tried and tested set of tools and materials to offer the opportunity to others. You don't have to be a sales person or even have any sales experience. You don't have to embellish what you're given in any way. All you need to be able to do is talk to people in their language – and this is easy if you're talking to your existing network.'

If you're wishing to make the transition from full time employment to part time business ownership that will over time give you a reliable passive income, then MLM could suit you very well.

But I'll give the final word to Andy:

'If you want to achieve more than 40-40-40 – that is spending forty years working forty hours a week and then living off forty per cent of what you could never live off in the first place – then MLM is for you.

'If you want more out of life, are prepared to listen to your mentor, put in the effort to achieve it, and Keep It Simple, then give it a go.'

Andy is happy to be contacted to share his knowledge about MLM. Find his contact details in the reference section at the back of the book.

So now for a reality check.

You might well be screaming, 'Stop! I have no money to start with. This is all a waste of time!'

If you are, don't worry. It's normal. I hear it all the time. And it should not be something that stops you. You don't need money to make money; there is always the opportunity to use other people's!

The easiest way to do this is to take out a loan; a bank loan, personal loan, mortgage etc. Borrowing to invest is not something I actively encourage. But if you can be sure that the return you are going to get is greater than the loan repayments you're going to have to make, it could make sense. Never borrow to gamble though!

So now you might be shouting, 'My credit rating is shot, I can't borrow!'

It's still not a problem. You don't need a lot of money to get going. Would a friend lend you some money? Your parents or other relatives? Just £100?

Where there is a will, there is always a way. You're not falling for your own excuses are you?

Reflective questions

- What can you do for thirty minutes every day to move you further towards your financial goal?
- What savings can you identify right now from your personal finances?
- What's your POTS Model strategy for your new-found savings?
- Who do you need on your team for help and guidance?
- What's your strategy for recruiting to your support team?
- Where will you meet the people you need?
- By when will you meet them?
- How will you keep track of your progress?

NOTES

[Page left blank for your reflections]

12

Mentors or meddlers: Who do you need to help you?

As your financial understanding deepens, and as you become more conscious of the illusory nature of much of the received wisdom promoted by The System and by all of your friends who would advise you against things that look 'too good to be true', you are becoming more open to the experiences of others who have already trodden the path to financial freedom before you.

Travelling alone can be tough. In the words of Winnie the Pooh – 'It's always much nicer with two.' No matter what our goals or ambitions in life it is often much more fulfilling and reassuring to know that there are like-minded others to guide us, and from whom we can learn.

In Section One I painted a picture of The System as a self-serving entity, deploying rules, regulations and rates of return that are intended to sustain itself rather than help you become rich.

The majority of the individuals involved in delivering regulated financial services are most likely acting in good faith. They would be appalled to think that they are duping any of their clients, and their professional knowledge about the packages and products they represent is most likely shared honestly and with good intent.

However, the fact remains that no matter how professional and well-intentioned the people involved in the financial services industry are, they are enacting policies and procedures biased in favour of The System they represent as opposed to the individual being served.

Some key questions to ask your financial advisor are:

- How are they remunerated?
- From where does their fee get taken – from your capital or from the returns?
- For every product or package they recommend to you, what's in it for them?

- How much of their own money are they investing in the products they represent?
- What's their level of understanding about the Alternatives' market?
- How much of their own money are they investing in Alternatives?

Head shaking and teeth sucking in response to the notion of Alternatives are likely signs of received ignorance rather than clear understanding. The retail investor is perpetually peddled the myth that Alternatives are dodgy investments, despite the fact that most people have bought property (itself classed as an Alternative investment) and benefited from using other people's money in the form of a mortgage in order to fund their purchase.

Nor does the average man on the street fully appreciate how the financial industry itself makes huge returns on Alternative investments. Typically we are also peddled the myth that sane people don't touch Alternatives with a barge pole, and that these products are classically 'too good to be true', despite the fact that the banks routinely use our money to leverage its own profits on the Alternatives' market. If you are talking to a financial advisor who refuses to acknowledge that regulated institutions make the majority of their profit from Alternatives – such as hedge funds and derivatives, and furthermore would avoid making such investments with their own money

– then it is likely they are as deluded by The System as the next man on the street.

Once the blinkers have fallen from your eyes on this point, and you can clearly recognise the regulatory structures for exactly what they are rather than what they purport to be, then you can be far more selective about the individuals whose help you seek.

The main message here is that the regulated market is financed largely by the profits made in Alternatives. So find people who understand this, and who can help you cut out the middle man.

Here's the case of Mike, the mortgage advisor with a difference.

Case Study: Mike

I first met Mike Hiner when he relocated his business to Royal Wootton Bassett, the town where I'm based. The same guy who manages my IT and technical set up was also involved in sorting out Mike's IT – and he thought the two of us should meet. That was some networking by a network specialist!

Mike's specialisms are mortgage brokerage and financial protection products, as well as providing consultancy on wills, trusts, and pension auto enrolment. As an appointed representative of an Financial Conduct Authority regulated network,

Mike's mortgage and protection business has the backing of the FCA.

The mere breadth of Mike's professional service offering, from mortgages to all types of life and business insurance, wills, probate and trusts, indicates a financial professional who is keen to engage with his clients on more than a transactional basis.

When Mike and I met he already had an interest in Alternative investments, and had dabbled a little, though couldn't really see how to turn them into a sustainable business alongside his regulated services.

Furthermore, he saw that those promoting Alternatives did it with more Del Boy hustle than calm confidence.

'The commission-driven used car salesman approach, and the sense that the deal is going to be here one minute and gone the next, is what the public most fear about Alternatives. But this hustling style does exist and it doesn't do any favours for the sector. It feeds into people's suspicions, as well as fuelling the scare-mongering efforts of the regulators.'

Mike and I sat down and worked through his five year plan, identifying where he wanted to get to and what life would look like for him and his fiancée.

'When I learned about Neil's approach at My Goal Is I immediately saw how getting to know his clients' aims and objectives, and helping them begin their journey with the end in mind, was a much more professional and sustainable approach than my first Alternatives' introducer had taken.

'It also aligned with my own preferred way of building loyalty in my client base, which goes beyond the transactional business so typical of many brokers and advisors.'

Mike is clear that when an advisor or introducer needs your investment in order to earn them their commission then alarm bells should ring. But it would be a mistake to attribute this type of sales approach to the Alternatives' sector alone. With an understanding of both regulated and unregulated markets, Mike is adamant that financial operators under FCA control can be just as unscrupulous.

To illustrate this point, he describes his disgust when he learned that one of his clients had been duped by a High Street building society.

'My client was an elderly lady who had been advised to invest £15,000 in a five year savings scheme. I'm not sure what returns were forecast at the outset but after the policy matured she received no more than her initial capital amount back.

'You could say that she was lucky not to lose her capital too, but that's not really the point. She was hoping to grow her fund not just put it somewhere for safe-keeping. There can be no doubt that the building society in question made a tidy profit investing her money to boost its own coffers. Not only did they not share the returns with her, they didn't tell her what they were doing with her pot each and every night. Yes it was growing – but for the building society, not the customer.'

This is a point that Mike is particularly keen for his clients and Alternatives' prospects to understand. The System itself makes huge profits out of unregulated products using savers' money without asking, and then sharing minuscule interest payments out of the spoils.

Since Mike and I first spoke I've been able to access an opportunity that makes investors returns of five per cent every month. From there he has gone on to introduce others to the same packages, and make a reliable residual income on his referrals' investments too.

'Mike's own five year plan really started to gain traction once he got involved with foreign exchange arbitrage.

'The FOREX opportunity took more of a leap of faith. It's a speculative investment with a fixed return of five per cent a month, which to many sounds too good to be true. But I understood that this is more the order of returns that banks and building societies regularly make on our deposits overnight, as they were doing with my elderly client's £15k, so all I was doing was cutting out the middle man to grow my cash.

'I overcame any misgivings I may have had by getting to know the fund administrator. Then when the payments started to hit my account like clockwork every quarter I was soon able to relax.'

So does Mike believe that retail investors can have independent and low-risk access to both regulated and unregulated markets?

Without doubt.

'It's such a myth that there is a world of difference and risk between regulated and unregulated markets. So many IFAs will flatly refuse to discuss Alternatives, but this is more likely out of ignorance than anything else, as well as the fear that any talk of unregulated products could cost them their authorisation.

'I keep my regulated and unregulated businesses separate, and never offer advice on Alternatives. But I can speak to curious clients about the opportunities in Alternatives, and I can show them the returns I'm making on my own money.'

Another thing that marks Mike out from other financial service practitioners is his ability to challenge his clients on what they wish to achieve. The reason why he and I clicked was because a strong motivation of his is to help his clients understand the consequences of their financial decisions and guide them in their financial education.

'Without this challenging approach we just perpetuate financial ignorance and deny people the opportunity to see the bigger picture,' Mike explains.

And there's a further way that Mike is a mortgage broker with a difference.

'Ironically, I don't actually have a mortgage myself. In fact, I rent my house!

'So many first time buyers come to me looking for a good mortgage deal, and with their hard-earned deposits burning a hole in their pocket. They are invariably young, and struggling financially, but they are absolutely desperate to get on the property ladder. This is mainly down to conditioning. We still subscribe to the myth that our homes are our biggest asset – when in reality they are our biggest liability!

'People are conditioned to think that renting is dead money. But I choose to take a different view, which is: why make the choice to pour all your capital into a property you can't really afford, nor really want to live in, just to get on the property ladder, and hopefully save up enough equity to eventually buy your dream house? Why not find your dream house now and rent it, while putting your capital into a mechanism that will not only grow it but also deliver you an income to amply cover the costs of your rent?

'That way, you can acquire the lifestyle and location you want right now – while you still have the energy to enjoy them.'

Sadly, though, most of Mike's clients are already sold on the idea of their dream home that will have them mortgaged to the hilt and cause them to start resenting it when they realise they can no longer afford to live life the way they wish to.

'This type of resentment and financial struggle then begins to spill over into other areas of life, such as our relationships, and suddenly the dream can rapidly turn into a nightmare.'

I believe Mike is one of a new breed of financial professionals who are truly dedicated to the success of their clients. His approach to business exemplifies how regulated and unregulated markets can coexist for the regular investor, in order to achieve more honest and profitable returns. He can demonstrate that he has his own money invested in opportunities that he is able to introduce to his clients, and he is able to debunk much of the misinformation about Alternative products.

But the best part of Mike's story is that in 2016 he will be using the interest payments from one of his investments to pay for his wedding.

Here's to his happy ever after!

Reflective questions

- What questions are you itching to find the answers to?
- Who do you need to talk to to get the answers you seek?
- What has surprised you?
- What has motivated you?
- What's next for you?

NOTES

[Page left blank for your reflections]

13

Mobility: Where can I live?

Being financially free enables you to travel and be flexible in your location. With no worries about having to exchange time for money you are free to spend your time wherever and however you choose.

This may involve relocating. Or it may involve travelling, or spending extended periods living away from home.

Christine and I love road trips, and the freedom of taking our motorhome to tour the British Isles and Europe. Our passive income enables us to decide how long we want to be away for, rather than how long we can afford to be away.

The rise of the Internet and social media has spawned a laptop lifestyle, where people can communicate and conduct their business effectively from any location. So if you are building a network of business colleagues through whom you are generating residual income, or if you are analysing stocks and shares and moving your money electronically, you never need to be disconnected. You can stay in contact with the things that are most important to you from wherever you choose to be.

'Never buy what you can rent'

Linked to this is another trademark mindset of the wealthy which states: 'Never buy what you can rent.'

It's worth putting the wisdom of this statement to the test. Clearly renting has to be more cost effective in the long term than ownership. You might not consider buying something you only used occasionally – like a power tool or a wedding tux or a holiday villa – but if the item was something you were likely to make use of multiple times then you are more likely to decide to bear the cost of it yourself.

For example, having worked out the cost of repeatedly renting a motor home, versus the one-off cost of purchasing one, it obviously makes more sense for us to own the vehicle ourselves; not to mention the sense of convenience and freedom it gives us to decide at the last minute that we fancy cutting loose for a weekend.

This may be too simplistic a concept, and I'm sorry if you feel like I'm teaching you to suck eggs. However, there is an important distinction to be made between 'bearing a cost' and 'making an investment'.

If you bear the cost of something you accept that it is an expense item for your own personal use. You do not expect it to generate any income for you. You do expect that it is likely to incur more cost. In order to use our van we have to spend money on fuel, maintenance, insurance and road tax. But this is money we can cover ourselves through saving on air fares and hotel bills that we no longer need to pay. In the bigger picture the cost of ownership is still less than the cost of occasional travel.

Were we to decide to *invest* in a motor home, we would have to cover the cost of ownership through other people's money. In order for it to be a true investment it would also have to make a profit and thus give us a return on our capital. In this sense it would become an income-generating asset rather than a cost-incurring liability. We would effectively be creating a motor home rental business, enabling others to benefit occasionally from the touring lifestyle without having to bear the cost of ownership for themselves.

So how is all this relevant to the idea of location and mobility?

In the UK people have traditionally aspired to owning their own home. The UK economy dictates that your home is the biggest 'investment' you will ever make, and the majority of people view getting onto the property ladder as a significant step in their financial security and independence.

But what if this is an illusion? What if property is far from the asset we tend to believe?

Think about it. Once you have secured your home through a mortgage and you have moved in to the property, when is the next time that so-called asset pays you any income?

More likely, our home is a money-pit. Heating, lighting, water, council tax, insurance and the costs of maintenance, decoration, comfort, convenience and security all add up. As well as paying your monthly loan repayments to the mortgage lender you are also liable for all the costs of living there.

The only way you will retrieve your capital, hopefully at a profit, will be to sell it and move. But then it wouldn't be your home anymore. So describing our home as our biggest asset might not be entirely accurate.

With this in mind, does it make more sense to rent rather than own your home?

The tenet 'Never buy what you can rent' needs further qualification. If you are investing in an income generating asset – a buy-to-let property or a business opportunity – then you are going to make a return on your outlay, so it may be better to buy. Likewise, if you are going to be making repeated use of something such that the cost of renting multiple times becomes unsustainable, then you may also be minded to buy. Please note that an expense reaches an unsustainable level when it demands more of your monthly cash than you can repeatedly afford. If, however, your cash-flow can sustain it and you don't want the hassle of ownership yourself, rent away. Just be clear on the ownership choices you're making and why you are making them.

Here's the case of Pet and Eva, a couple who are living the dream abroad.

Case Study: Pete and Eva

I first met Pete and Eva in February 2014 after they had been referred to me by a networking colleague who is an accountant and international tax advisor.

Pete and Eva are a young, professional couple: he's an accomplished engineer and she an author, therapist and natural health specialist. They love rock-climbing and the outdoors: but at the time we met their work was keeping them away from each other – and from the things they love.

Explaining how they were both getting itchy feet in their jobs, Eva said:

'Whilst I was working from home, Pete was doing a daily commute to a city thirty miles away. During the week we'd only have a couple of hours in the evening to spend quality time together. At the weekends we might get to do some climbing but we'd always have to make time to do the laundry and get ready for the following week's work.

'I started to think – hang on a minute, this is not how I want to spend my time and my life.'

A strong and driven personality, Eva has always been convinced that she would achieve financial independence by the age of fifty, and has worked hard in her profession to get ahead, securing a doctorate and writing books to help others turn their health around.

'When we met Neil we already had a vision of what we wanted to achieve,' Eva explained. 'Or at least what we thought we wanted to achieve.'

It's good that the couple were starting with the end in mind, having produced a vision board and creating a goal to work towards. However, there were a couple of things in their approach which were slightly off – and which unbeknown to them at the time were possibly holding them back.

The couple's goal at the time was to build a bed and breakfast retreat centre in the mountains of Eva's native Poland. Their vision board was crammed with stunning vistas, beautiful landscapes and serene interiors, reflecting their ideal environment in which to host guests.

But their first mistake was perhaps the preconception that in order to build a property that would be big enough to generate an income to live on they would need a huge injection of capital which they didn't yet have.

Eva started explaining:

'I've always believed that the thing you need will turn up as long as you remain open-minded and receptive. So even though our friends were all asking us how on earth we would find the money to fund our vision I never lost faith. I spoke to everyone I met about what Pete and I were looking to do – and that's when the accountant I met at a networking event told me we needed to speak to Neil.'

Taking up the story, Pete said:

'When we went to meet Neil for the first time I remember saying to Eva that I wasn't sure how worthwhile it was going to be. We had worked out our plan, and thought we knew what it was going to take to get there.

'As Neil began to explain what was possible I remember thinking how surreal it was. Once we understood what strategies were open to us we realised that we didn't have to wait for the perfect lump sum of capital to become available.

'Suddenly the whole project came into real focus and we discovered that we could start creating the life we longed for a lot sooner than we had imagined.'

But the prospect of being able to bring their dream forward presented the couple with a new set of uncertainties.

'We had bought the perfect plot of land and identified how we could begin to finance our project – but then we started to ask ourselves why we wanted to build and run the centre in the first place,' said Eva. 'Then we discovered that the Polish mountains are mined for uranium. This was a bit of a show-stopper since we didn't want to be sending climbers up radioactive rock-faces!'

The couple had to go back to the drawing board to a certain degree, but Pete reckoned this was an important part of the journey.

He said: 'It was one of the things that forced us to re-evaluate what we wanted. The other thing was the fact that our investment portfolio was giving us a big enough income to live on. Suddenly the idea of running a business that enabled other people to do what we loved doing, instead of being able to do it ourselves, felt a bit daft.'

Pete and Eva were discovering an important principle of the journey to financial freedom: that although their vision had got them moving, the route they would take would never go straight from A to B.

'I work with people's values and beliefs all the time, and how these conflict,' said Eva. 'But it wasn't until we were in the position to be able to build our dream that we started to see how being responsible for a big business was not quite what we had in mind. We value our time spent outdoors but we believed we had to work hard to achieve more of it for ourselves. In a nutshell we came face to face with our own conflicting values and beliefs!'

Soon the idea of a Polish retreat centre, with its brutal winters, lost its appeal.

'Again our focus was sharpening. Often it's hard to know what you really want until you are presented with choices.

'We didn't want to be tied to working if we didn't have to, and we preferred the idea of a more temperate climate than the Polish mountains would offer,' Pete said.

'So in October 2015 we moved to northern Spain!'

Their trajectory certainly took a sharp detour, but being flexible, open-minded people they found it easy to adapt to a new plan of action.

Pete and Eva were learning that moving towards financial freedom can bring surprising changes to one's outlook and perceptions. They were also experiencing at first hand lots of nay-saying from friends and family.

'Most people we spoke to about moving to Spain had only one question for us – which was what would we do for work,' said Pete.

'At first we tried to explain that we would be running an online business, which is sort of true as Eva still writes and publishes books and courses that are available on the Internet, but really it was a way of avoiding telling people that actually we didn't have to work.'

'Yes and this really started to bug me!' interjected Eva. 'I got curious about why we find it so difficult to say 'I don't have to work,' and why I was trying to hide what we do. So I stopped.

'People make a lot of assumptions because they don't know what's possible, or because they don't want to know.'

After searching over 60 properties throughout Spain they eventually found their ideal base an hour outside Alicante. At the moment a typical day for them includes painting, decorating, planting trees, sorting out the vegetable garden and learning to maintain their swimming pool!

Pete explained: 'We feel like we are building a new quality of life here. Eva is always going to want to contribute to her field and in a couple of years we will perhaps revisit the idea of a smaller scale retreat business. But instead of a big hotel we'll build a couple of independent apartments on our land.'

Eva feels very strongly that her work as a therapist must not be tied to making money. She said: 'As soon as you need the work to make money your credibility and integrity diminish. Having our income generated by our investment portfolio is very liberating, and means that I can be a better therapist for my clients.'

Over the course of two years this young couple have learned a huge amount about themselves and about what's possible. By starting with the end in mind, being receptive to new ideas and changes, and being clear about who they are becoming, they have achieved their dream life in a remarkably short time.

EPILOGUE TO SECTION TWO

Your life will never be the same once you embark on your financial freedom journey. You are giving yourself opportunities and understanding that the vast majority of people never have.

Once you have set the flywheel in motion, keep your eye on it and it will spin under its own momentum, with only gentle guidance and the odd nudge from you.

By way of a conclusion, here's a checklist of To Dos. Test yourself against each item to see how much you now understand in comparison to before you picked up this book. How far have you come already?

- Educate yourself – ask the right questions
- Distinguish fact from opinion, illusion from reality
- Choose who you wish to become
- Begin with the end in mind
- Understand your attitude to risk – and expect it to change
- Commit to the POTS Model
- Grasp the Compound Effect – and respect it!
- Protect your capital at all costs
- Conduct a due diligence process for every opportunity

- Build a trusted network
- Leverage others' time, money, knowledge and skills as much as possible
- Stay curious and open-minded

LEAP OF FAITH

In *The Last Crusade*, Indiana Jones encounters one of his toughest challenges – to make a death defying leap of faith across an underground ravine. As he stands on the rocky ledge he consults his map that directs him to the opposite ledge, twenty five metres away.

'There's no way I can jump that,' he tells himself breathlessly, but then hears the cries of his father deep down in the cavern. He needs to do something urgently.

He resolves to take a leap of faith. In a heart-stopping moment he takes a deep breath, closes his eyes, places his hand on his chest and extends his leg out away from the relative safety of the ledge.

In seconds his foot comes to rest on a solid structure extending away from the ledge. Gradually he comes to the realisation that he has stepped on to an invisible bridge. Gingerly he makes his way across the bridge, which becomes visible to him as he progresses. It is narrow and uneven, and requires careful navigation.

Finally, Indy is able to jump onto the opposite ledge, where he stoops, collects some sand and throws it back over the bridge, so he will be able to see it on his return.

Many people will not make the leap of faith that is required for their financial freedom. Perhaps they are too wrapped up in the old financial dogma. They don't get it. More importantly they don't have Steven Spielberg directing them to step on to a bridge they cannot see, urging them to do the courageous, adventurous thing for the sake of their best life. Instead they have the scaremongering propaganda of self-interested institutions warning them away from the edge, persuading them that there is no invisible bridge to bear their weight.

I'm making no claims to be an Indiana Jones. Hats and whips don't particularly suit me. But I do know that there is a bridge you can cross to financial freedom, and that many people have crossed it before you.

My greatest hope is that this book can be like Indy's handful of sand to make the bridge visible to you as you cross.

GLOSSARY

Capital	Cash. The funds you use to create income.
Financial freedom	You have achieved financial freedom when you have no debt, and your income for the rest of your life comes entirely from passive investments.
Passive income	Income you receive without having to exchange it for your time.
Protect your capital at all costs	This means keeping the full amount of your investment cash intact, and taking income from the returns it makes. It also implies spreading the risk and not putting all your eggs into one basket.
Resources	Time, money, knowledge, experience, contacts – anything you can put to use to help you achieve your financial goal.
Retirement	Sacking the boss,

	stopping exchanging time for money. Doesn't just have to happen in your fifties or sixties!
Return	The total figure at the end of the period of investment, less the initial capital you put in
The System	The varied institutions that conspire to keep us towing the line, exchanging time for money, paying our taxes and accepting low returns on our financial investments; including: education, government, media, financial industry.
Work	Exchanging time for money.

FURTHER READING

- Property Magic – Simon Zutshi
- Rich Dad Poor Dad – Robert Kiyosaki
- The Slight Edge – Jeff Olson
- The Chimp Paradox – Dr Steve Peters
- Everything You Need you Have – Gerad Kite

NEXT STEPS

- Visit our website: www.mygoalis.uk.com
- Watch the Educational Videos: www.mygoalis.uk.com/mgi-resources
- Download the Financial Freedom Planner: www.mygoalis.uk.com/mgi-resources
- Complete the Online Assessment form: www.mygoalis.uk.com/online-assessment
- Contact us: 01793 858215 or service@mygoalis.uk.com

Printed in Great Britain
by Amazon